ARTS & LETTERS

ARTS & LETTERS

EDITOR	LAURA NEWBERN
FICTION EDITOR	CHIKA UNIGWE
NONFICTION EDITOR	PETER SELGIN
POETRY EDITOR	KERRY JAMES EVANS
MANAGING EDITOR	DARIAN ARAIZA-SAMPLES
ASSISTANT MANAGING EDITOR	CAS MCKINNEY
ASSISTANT EDITORS	MER ALSOBROOKS
	SHANNON YARBROUGH
	TIM CONNORS
	COURTNEY SCHMIDT
	DENECHIA POWELL
ART DIRECTOR	PETER SELGIN
FOUNDING EDITOR	MARTIN LAMMON

Arts & Letters is published twice a year at Georgia College

Copyright © 2022 Georgia College
Printed at Sheridan Press
Hanover, PA
ISSN 1523-4592

ArtsAndLetters.gcsu.edu
@ArtsLettersGC

Many thanks to:

Dr. Barry Darugar for all his generous support over the years of the Arts & Letters / Rumi Prize for Poetry.

Bahram and Fari Atefat, for their generous gift to endow the Arts & Letters/Susan Atefat Prize in Creative Nonfiction, to honor the memory of their daughter Susan and grandson Cyrus.

And the judges for this year's prizes:
Allison Joseph • Andrew Porter • Gayle Brandeis

ANNUAL PRIZE WINNERS

FICTION

POETRY

NONFICTION

FLASH

JODIE NOEL VINSON

ARTS & LETTERS / SUSAN ATEFAT PRIZE FOR CREATIVE NONFICTION

FIRST DO NO HARM

I.

Florence Nightingale, as portrayed by a children's biography I was given in elementary school, was a feminine creature, "the lady with the lamp;" she who was never a mother was called the "mother of modern nursing," a comfort to fallen soldiers. We weren't told about her analytical brain, or about the over 200 books, pamphlets and reports that secured her place as the first woman admitted to the Royal Statistical Society. I never knew her pursuit of a career that attracted working class women upset her bourgeois family, who preferred she stay at home. *Cassandra*, 22-year-old Nightingale's attempt at a novel, is a thinly veiled autobiographical account of a Victorian family's constraint on a young woman's freedom. I never read it, but Virginia Woolf did. "It is hardly writing," she'd observe. "It is more like screaming."

When she finally left home on assignment in the Crimean War, Nightingale was sent to Scutari, where rat-infested barracks had been converted into a make-shift hospital. "The men, and even their wounds, swarmed with vermin…they lay…in indescribable filth," journalist Harriet Martineau reported in an account written with Nightingale to raise the public's awareness of the need for healthcare reform. In this narrative, the famous nurse appears not as administering angel, but as a helpless cog caught in a bureaucratic machine.

II.

I arrive at the vaccination clinic early, but the sun is already hot, reflected off the blacktop mirror that surrounds the concrete edifice. Against the broad, flat face of the building, flakes of white cling to the swimsuit tan of five letters.

I'm volunteering at the clinic because a year earlier I was sicker than I ever have been. Because, a year later, my body is still recovering. The day I boarded the plane to visit my sister in India, the first death by coronavirus was recorded in the U.S. Over the span of my two-week holiday, the world changed. The day of my return flight, Trump declared a travel ban on non-U.S. citizens. A few hours before boarding, I emptied my stomach in every bathroom in the baggage claim of the Delhi airport.

Over the weeks following my return, my symptoms worsened, but the shortage of hospital beds kept me home. As Covid cases surged in New York, the Javitz Convention Center was lined with close to 3,000 cots; an ice rink in Spain became a morgue. Field hospitals were erected in sports stadiums and college dorm rooms, on state fairgrounds, even inside a parking garage. I waited. But while my case was mild, it was also mysteriously long. When, three months after the initial infection, the intermittent pains in my chest sharpened, my husband drove me to the ER.

I pull open a set of double glass doors and submit to a temperature check. I'm here, I remind myself, because I may have contributed to the disease's spread, and feel responsible for the lives that continue to be lost. In a way, you could see the hours I spend checking people in and out of a clinic housed in a defunct Sears department store on the borders of town I don't even live in as a sort of penance.

III.

Sacrifice was an integral part of the ancient healing process, as were religious rites like prayer and dream interpretation, which occurred alongside the setting of bones and stitching of wounds. Some of the earliest healthcare facilities were housed in temples consecrated to gods of medicine, such as Asclepius, a Greek deity who revealed himself in dreams, which, once interpreted by a priest, pointed to a cure. Plans for a temple dedicated to the god in the fifth century BC outline what might be called one of the earliest known hospital wards—a large open room designed for several patient-dreamers, who, on a clear day, might step out among the columns into a sunlit courtyard.

When the Greeks entered Egypt under Alexander the Great, they would recognize the Egyptian god Imhotep as that dream-frequenter of their own pantheon. Two thousand years ahead of Hippocrates, Imhotep had documented close to 50 injuries and treatments in hieroglyphic scrawl. On the reverse of the papyrus, as if for good measure, he appended eight magic spells and several healing chants.

Before his apotheosis, Imhotep was the first human to build with stone, constructing a step pyramid in Sakhara that spurned the conventional conical form to rise in five diminishing steps to 204 feet—the tallest structure of its time. The pyramid was commissioned as a tomb for a pharaoh, who, after his internment under its auspices, was to become a god. Imhotep achieved his own immortal status centuries later when humanity's first known architect was deified as the god of healing.

Not all the ancients believed illnesses were sent by the gods, or that they could be healed by spoken spells, or even their dreams. Hippocrates, Father of Medicine, would use observation to categorize disease, make prognosis and prescribe treatment. Though raised in a family of physician priests, Hippocrates left the temple of Asclepius to establish his own school of medicine, with an oath today's med students still swear by.

IV.

"It may seem a strange principle to enunciate as the very first requirement in a Hospital that it should do the sick no harm," Nightingale would echo Hippocrates in *Notes on Hospitals*, her 1863 treatise on hospital design. On the Crimean War front, where more British soldiers were dying from disease contracted in the hospital than from bullets, she'd seen the consequences of a poorly conceived sick unit. Back then, it was necessary not only to emphasize the positive, active principles of healing but also to exclude the negative, harmful effects of a passive or even neglectful environment. Case in point: Nightingale's more famous *Notes on Nursing* is subtitled *What It is, and What It is Not.*

Notes on Hospitals was predicated on medical theories of the time, such as miasma—the belief that diseases were carried by invisible, noxious fumes. But Nightingale's designs were also based on observations about the way humans interact with their lived environment. Despite Hippocrates' efforts to divorce healing from the gods, in the nineteenth century, healthcare facilities were often associated with religious institutions. While wealthy and middle-class patients stayed home even for surgery, the state of such almshouses was often poor, with patients crowded into unventilated rooms on the outskirts of cities and towns.

Nightingale's hospital plans advocated for a pavilion design that isolated the sick in wards with windows looking out on a courtyard or landscape. She knew her patients in rooms facing east recovered more quickly than those without access to the sun, noting, "It is a curious thing to observe how almost all patients lie with their faces turned to the light, exactly as plants always make their way towards the light." *Notes on Nursing* is peppered with such pithy and even punchy aphorisms, crafted to reach the working class while appealing to the wit of the educated. "There is nothing yet discovered which is a substitute to the English patient for his cup of tea;" she quips, for example: "he can take it when he can take nothing else, and he often can't take anything else if he has it not."

In a satirical nineteenth century engraving, a lady of society drops a tea cup as she peers through a telescope, at the end of which balloons a microcosm of her view: a circle crawling with skeletal sea monsters, creeping crawdads and fanged centipedes—all inhabitants, the viewer understands, of her tea. Germ theory had begun to take hold of the public's imagination, driven by experiments by men of science like Louis Pasteur. While proponents of miasma held that infection stemmed from particles released by decomposing materials, Pasteur demonstrated how the microbes identified in his lab were the cause of disease, and not the result.

Nightingale resisted germ theory, rejecting hospital plans that made room for laboratories. She was concerned that, by giving way to this new science, something would be lost of the remedies she'd found so effective. Of course, in her efforts to sanitize and brighten hospitals, the nurse's reforms had inadvertently done away with germs, just as germ theory, by relegating disease transmission to an interaction between a microorganism and a host, would do away with practices whose basis may have been in an overturned principle, and yet were, in Nightingale's view, no less worthy: the bright contrast of color a bedside bouquet brought to a whitewashed room; fresh air blown by a breeze through an open window, stirring the currents before drawn into a patient's lungs; the natural warmth of a ray of light.

V.

A petite woman in fatigues, hair pulled back severely in a low bun, strides past my check-in table at the vaccination clinic, hands interlaced behind her back, boots clicking self-importantly on a linoleum path that loops the perimeter of the former department store. Florescent lights covered by rectangles of plastic douse everything in a bright, even luminescence without drawing attention to the source. The space is echoy, tan, hard, and vast. There is no evidence of what the company once advertised as "the softer side of Sears."

The store is also vaguely familiar. When I'd arrived at the ER months earlier to investigate ongoing Covid symptoms, I hadn't been in a hospital as a patient since birth, and—judging by the beige and pink curtains that hung in my room—the décor hadn't been updated since the 80s. The curtains hung over the only feature of the room that might be called a window—a wall of glass that looked into the interior of the hospital, where nurses were stationed behind a large circular desk. I felt as if I'd entered another world, shut off from the one in which my husband—barred by Covid regulations from entering the ER—would wait in the parking lot for the next seven hours, sometimes pacing up and down the block, where the neighborhood's trees were beginning to display the full extent of their leafy green foliage.

A single rectangular panel glowed over my hospital bed from the low ceiling, which I had a good chance to examine as I lay leashed by several wires to the heart monitor beeping over my shoulder. Icy fluid coursed from the IV into my veins, but there were no blankets on my bed. Someone had drawn the ugly curtains across the glass wall, blocking my view of personnel I could hear moving outside. When someone came to escort me to a CT scan, I was almost in tears — not from any ailment, but because of the sheer discomfort of the situation.

Wheeled on my bed through a dim warren of hospital halls, I watched ceiling tiles pass overhead, interspersed with flashes of fluorescence. Admitted on my back into a dusky room with the feel of a hushed theater, I was aware of an audience somewhere behind glass; otherwise I was alone. Just past my toes rose a donut-shaped machine, ominous portal to another world. I'd gone underground, or to another planet, and if kept here much longer, I might soon forget the sun.

VI.

The insistent clip of boots on tile brings me back to the clinic, patrolled by the vigilant National Guardsman. Halfway down the length of one wall, the linoleum path widens into a circle where the flooring becomes rough with a jagged layer of concrete, as if a heavy fixture had been torn from the spot. For a moment, I see a brightly lit circular display, a slim woman rising above it. Below her demonstrative hands delicate chains, diamond rings, and gleaming gold watches wink under warm lights.

In 1886 a railway car filled with pocket watches rolled into the Minnesota station where Richard W. Sears worked as a station agent. When the shipment was refused by its intended buyer, Sears purchased the watches at a discount, then sold them for a profit. By the late 1890s Sears and his partner Roebuck had developed a 300-page mail order catalog to serve rural Americans eager for consumer goods. Advertising everything from firearms to pre-fab kit homes, the Sears catalog was so ubiquitous it became a euphemism for toilet paper.

As its rural customers migrated to cities, Sears department stores began to appear at the edges of urban centers. True to his initial calling, the former station agent bought up lots at the crossroads outside of towns, erecting large, spacious stores on discounted land that would become, in the following decades, the suburbs.

A century later, my sisters and I would accompany my mom on shopping excursions in our suburban town in Iowa, following her cart around Targets and Walmarts, Sears and JC Penneys, Kohls and the occasional Kmart—single-story structures built on a slab of concrete surrounded by a sweeping expanse of blacktop. Inside, selling floors were merchandized in a loop layout that circled the store like a racetrack, maximizing windowless wall space and exposing us to rows of discounted products before, cart full, we found ourselves back at check out.

At home, we'd cut out paper dolls from the thin models in pastel sweaters who arrived in the pages of our hefty Sears catalogs. Scissoring around thin torsos and cocked hips, we freed beautiful women and blue-eyed men from the small print and prices, acting out domestic scenes across the carpet, the passion of our play vaguely fueled by a strange desire rising from the glossy pages of the catalog.

Initially the products my sisters and I coveted in our catalog were fit into the company's brick-and-mortar stores. But soon Sears was designing stores to display the merchandise, such as the Sears on Pico Boulevard in Los Angeles, the first to innovate with an open floor plan. In addition to the store's rooftop parking lot, the Pico Sears incorporated air conditioning and streamlined escalators—all in service of the selling floor. The store claimed the largest retail street level window in the city; otherwise the building was windowless.

VII.

As the organisms behind infectious diseases were revealed beneath microscopes, fresh air and sunlight began to fall out of focus as preventative healthcare. At some point in her career, even Nightingale came around to the presence of disease-causing pathogens, advising nurses to wash their hands with chlorinated soda. "It may destroy germs at the expense of the cuticle," she'd lark, "but if it takes off the cuticle, it must be bad for the germs."

Germ theory's reductive nature—doing away with environment, climate and other subjective influences to focus on a particle beneath a microscope—appealed to physicians whose social status was rising as medicine became a specialized practice that happened in the laboratory rather than the home. Instead of viewing a sick ward as a therapeutic means to health, hospitals began to be seen as backdrops for the real work of science. "At best, this modern hospital design proved an efficient tool for facilitating current medical behaviors and practices," writes Jeanne Kisacky in *The Rise of the Modern Hospital*, "at worst, it provided a cold, off-putting, chaotic space that aggrandized doctors and procedures, fetishized germs, and dehumanized patients."

Nightingale's pavilion-style hospitals would be replaced in the twentieth century by multi-floor blocks with a patient tower placed on top. This deep span of mega hospitals meant a lack of windows for interior rooms. "With the aid of air conditioning and deep span frame structures," W. Paul James would observe in his 1986 *Hospitals: Design and Development*, "it becomes possible to plan a hospital like a department store, in one continuous floor, occupying the whole of the site."

VIII.

Inside the shuttered Sears, the Guardsman stops her endless loops to ask if I'll train at check-out. I follow her across the sales floor to my new post, where another volunteer shows me how to scan each patient's receipt and record their vaccination in the system. Like the other volunteers, she's a few decades older than me, around retirement age, dressed in a navy T-shirt and khaki pants. New here, I'm in tight black jeans. Our monitors are set up next to each other at the end of lanes that extend out from the nurses' station. She's been caring for elderly parents at home for over a year, the volunteer tells me as she hands me a roll of "I'm Vaccinated!" stickers. We all have our reasons for being here, and I assume they are hers, but then she tells me her sister got Covid a few months ago and has yet to fully recover.

As the volunteer describes her sister's condition, I feel a momentary recognition. For months I'd held aloof from strangers, affronted by those who wouldn't wear masks or ate in restaurants while I still carried the effects of the long illness in my body. Though I often felt like screaming, I retreated with my aching lungs back into my apartment in silence, powerless to change the behavior of others. Now I find myself telling my fellow volunteer about the ongoing symptoms that followed my mild case. She looks at me over her N-95, nodding along. "Yeah, that's what happened to my sister. She got Covid. She was fine at first. And then she wasn't."

I'm grateful for her acknowledgment. A year earlier, when I first fell ill, few people would believe the symptoms of a 14-day disease could last this long. When my tests taken in the ER came back normal, I had trouble convincing anyone something was wrong. Without objective proof from the labs, it didn't take the doctors long to imply my symptoms were a result of my anxiety, and not the cause.

In the months following my trip to the ER, I'd passed in and out of exam rooms, claustrophobic cubes where waits were long and temperatures always arctic. By the time the doctor entered I was a bundle of nerves ready to confess to anything. I caved to their skepticism, cowered and acquiesced to their disbelief. I was so terrified of the sharp pains inside my chest I often cried, giving them cause to prescribe anxiety meds for symptoms they couldn't see.

One doctor suggested psychotherapy, another lectured on the origins of Greek medicine, tracing two circles in the air before sitting in the roller chair across from me. In her first circle floated the measurable effects of illness, perceived beneath the delicate glass of a microscope, identified in the chiaroscuro contours of an X-ray, ticked off in the measured rhythms of a heart monitor. In her second circle hung the more obscure, subjective symptoms of the body: here she placed my fatigue; here, she put my pain. Neither of the latter were useful, she clarified: "We can't base a diagnosis on that." But after months of illness, I didn't have much else to show. *The Greeks used to believe in patients' dreams*, I wanted to argue. *Now we don't even listen to their pain?*

The doctor's colorless eyes examined me as I described the compression in my chest, the tidal waves of weariness, my elevated pulse. But my insistence on illness only reinforced her final assessment. I watched her scribble an order for an anxiety medication I would never take. "First do no harm," the doctor defended her ineffectual prescription with her sacred oath.

Was Hippocrates ever sick? I wondered as I swung my feet to the linoleum floor, and headed to check out.

IX.

When I was in school, we weren't taught about Nightingale's ultimate sacrifice, about the disease, contracted on the front, that followed her home. We didn't learn Nightingale's initial illness was described by her doctor as the worst attack of Crimean fever he'd encountered. In photos I was shown, the nurse always looked pristine, skirt ballooning from corseted waist, iconic lantern raised, dark hair parted down the middle, thin features peeking out below the brim of a scarf or bonnet. I never saw images from when she shaved her head as a convalescent under the incessant heat of a Crimean sun. I didn't know when she wrote in *Notes on Nursing*, "the very walls of their sickrooms seem hung with their cares…the ghosts of their troubles haunt their beds," she was speaking from experience. They didn't tell us how her symptoms, which recurred with sporadic violence modern medicine attributes to a chronic form of brucellosis—a zoonotic illness often spread through goat's milk—would keep her, at the age of 35, bedridden and indoors for the next 30 years.

When Nightingale returned home from the war, her family couldn't recognize her; even her personality had been flattened by disease. We now know her symptoms, which included sciatica, breathlessness, tachycardia and depression, align with cases in which the causal agent—a bacterium known as *Brucella melitensis*—had been cultured from the blood. But without such proof of illness at the time, Nightingale's ongoing suffering would be doubted, disparaged and mis-diagnosed as "neurasthenia," an obsolete term for a psychosomatic nervous disorder—in other words, all in her head.

In insisting hospitals do no harm, Nightingale may have been borrowing from Hippocrates. But while the phrase "first do no harm" originated with the Greek physician, his words are often taken out of context. The axiom appears nowhere in the twelve-part Hippocratic Oath; rather, it occurs in *Of the Epidemics*, a treatise in which Hippocrates advises doctors to "have two special objects in view with regard to disease, namely, to do good or to do no harm." The negative, passive approach of doing no harm is never given priority over providing help to someone in pain.

The study of brucellosis was contemporary with Nightingale's malady. The bacterium at the root of Crimean fever was first identified by scientists in 1887, some 30 years after she first fell ill—and just as many of her symptoms seem to have abated. Eight years after Nightingale passed away in 1910, Dr. Alice Evans was infected with *Brucella melitensis* while working with a culture. Her symptoms, consistent with what Nightingale reported, were misdiagnosed as neurasthenia for six years until the organism was discovered in her blood—I imagine a sharp-toothed cartoon of a crawdad grinning up from the microscope slide. Seventeen years of illness followed.

In 1995 an article appeared in the *British Medical Journal* connecting Nightingale's ailments with chronic brucellosis, ending the tyranny of biographers, doctors and scholars who'd damaged her reputation as someone who falsified illness for her own means. "Patients with proved chronic brucellosis reported long delays before the correct diagnosis was made," David Young concludes his study, noting the interim diagnosis was almost always neurasthenia. The same was true for Nightingale, he observes, ending on a gross understatement: "Although a delay of 140 years seems excessive."

For those experiencing the long fallout of symptoms following a Covid infection, research has also been a step behind the disease's progress. In a capitalist society, science unfolds at the pace of money. That studies on Long Covid are happening at all is because the number of those with chronic symptoms is legion. Our suffering is profitable, and so we have hope of being heard, of discovering diagnostic proof of our pain, and of one day receiving treatment for it. Is it any wonder that in time of crisis, in place of sun-dappled temples and airy pavilions, our place of healing is a big box store?

X.

I emerged from that ER visit with no answers. Breathing in the night air, I peered through the dark toward the two bright beams in the parking lot that marked my husband's long vigil. Behind me the hospital loomed against the night sky, a hulking barge moored in a sea of pavement. What began with the fundraising efforts of a few Jewish women, led to a charitable hospital, which was replaced by this modern building designed to serve the entire community with efficiency and purpose after World War II. The hospital expanded over the decades into residential and commercial areas around its quiet neighborhood, eventually establishing a Cardiac Center in the basement level of a nearby vacant Sears department store.

In the decades following the Second World War, sales were at an all-time high; by 1970 Sears, Roebuck and Company was the largest retailer in the world. At this pinnacle of power, the company commissioned a skyscraper that would epitomize the heights of its success. Composed of enough concrete to make a five-mile long eight-lane highway, with 16,000 tinted windows, the 110-story building would be the world's tallest—until it wasn't.

From the heights of its skyscraper headquarters, Sears had a long way to fall, but in the face of internet sales and big box store competition from companies like Walmart, even its softer side couldn't save the retail business. By 2018, a towerless Sears had declared bankruptcy, shuttering stores across the country.

While the landmark Pico store was sold and torn down, another Los Angeles Sears would survive, becoming a temporary hospital for Riverside County. During the Covid-19 pandemic, the 90,000 square foot open floor plan would host 125 hospital beds. Some stores were razed to make room for parks and parking lots, entertainment venues and skating rinks. Others stand empty, yawning vestiges of a fallen empire.

XI.

Before bedridden, Nightingale had been a traveler. Her last trip, just after she'd turned down a suitable marriage proposal and just before she went into the trenches of Crimea, was a three-month journey along the Nile River. Turned inward, intent upon discovering her calling in life, the 29-year-old initially found the country's famous pyramids to be "vulgar" and "uninteresting," their most sublime attribute their size. The age-old monuments seemed to her "a form without beauty, without ideal, devised only to resist time, to last the longest."

There was one pyramid, however, that moved the traveler. Maybe it was how it stood out from the others—composed of five steps rather than the sheer sides of a cone. As she clamored up a mound to get a better view, Nightingale couldn't have known her opinion would one day be sought by architects around the world, that the king of Portugal would ask her advice on the hospital he wished built in memory of his wife. She could not have guessed her interests in nursing and design would intertwine to become the calling she sought in her journals as she traveled. But perhaps she sensed the roots of what would become her practice were manifest in the limestone steps of that pyramid in Sakhara, built by Imhotep, humanity's first architect, who would become a healing god.

Or maybe it was simply that, as she wrote, "the Pyramids lost their vulgarity—their come, look-at-me appearance, and melted away into a fitting part and portion of this vast necropolis." In any case, the harshness she'd first perceived "was softened away by the shadow of death, which reigned over the place — as moonlight makes everything look beautiful."

XII.

No one is good at small talk anymore. After our first exchange, the volunteer and I have been amiably silent as we pass out stickers and direct people to the observation area. During a lull in appointments, I look over. Before contracting Covid, I tell her, I'd thought of myself as a traveler. Now, tracing pathways of contact on a backwards journey through India, I find myself questioning what right I have to go where I wish. At what invisible cost? Recalling the cold symptoms that set in as I'd arrived in the country, I rehearse every interaction and relive each exchange. I see the faces of the drivers, cooks and caretakers who'd been my uncomplaining hosts, imagine the lives — and deaths — of the other passengers on that long flight home.

Nightingale's collapse after Crimea is attributed by some biographers unwilling to accept the organic nature of her illness as an overwhelming guilt over the lives lost at her hospital. The British government's efforts to cover up the shocking sanitary conditions that caused 16,323 of the Crimean War's 21,097 deaths didn't resolve Nightingale's sense of responsibility. Even if we accept her illness as real, this knowledge of lives lost by her actions — or inactions — could explain the nurse's inexhaustible push for reform from her sickbed, where, between endless reports and constant correspondence, her pen scrawled "never forget" across the blotting paper, again and again.

In the wake of the 1857 First War of Independence, Nightingale's attention turned from Crimea to India, where British troops were dying of cholera, as well as spreading the disease to the local populace. Though she longed to travel there, her health never permitted the trip. Instead Nightingale studied the country from her sick bed, compiling reports and papers, including one she called *How People May Live and Not Die in India*. "We do not care for the people of India," another begins, "Do we even care enough to know about their daily lives of lingering death from causes which we could do so well to remove?" The article was dismissed by the complacent British officials it implicated as a "shriek."

When I returned home from India, I was one of twenty known cases in my state. It's one thing to fall sick at the peak of a pandemic. Then, you're a victim, not an instigator. You are number 5,042 or 19,763 or number three million and one. But to have been, if not patient zero, one of twenty, to know your decisions might have stopped the spread, if you hadn't insisted on finishing your vacation, on filling your fridge. At what number is it still possible to prevent a pandemic? Unlike Nightingale, I'm not a statistician. But at some point we had the power to save the lives of the over five million who would follow. Like her, I can see there was no reason for those people to die.

I'd spend the next year and a half searching for a cure, moving between uniform exam rooms and in and out of online support groups for thousands afflicted by symptoms lingering after a Covid infection. Whenever my ongoing illness is disbelieved by doctors, I think of Nightingale. I imagine the nurse propped against pillows, writing from a bed that faces, of course, a window. I think about how it's possible to leave for a trip one person and come back another. About how it sometimes takes being a patient to become an advocate. I return, again and again, to the clinic in the abandoned Sears as I once might have gone to the marketplace, as a way of participating in society, as an acknowledgement that we are all connected, that our decisions — to get on a plane, to shop at a store, to wear a mask, to get the jab — have consequences on other lives; that to do no harm is never a passive decision, but an always active awareness.

Even from her sick bed, Nightingale was not idle. In 1860 she established a nursing school that would influence healthcare professionals across the globe. The nurses trained at St. Thomas Hospital, an institution that began in 1213 as an almshouse. At the time of the school's founding, St. Thomas was being purchased by a railway that wished to lay tracks through hospital grounds. While waiting for a new facility to be built in the suburbs, the hospital, with its nurses-in-training, took up temporary residence at a former zoo. The Giraffe House became the cholera ward; cadavers were studied where elephants once roamed.

As much as she contributed to their design, "hospitals," Nightingale once wrote, "are only an intermediate stage of civilization." Nursing, and its work of recovery, was to her a practice that transcended the compartmentalized world of medical science, a process that happened through all structures of society, within the home, and especially in relation to the natural world. Her work was to empower women with this knowledge, so that when the systems we depend upon fail us, we might, as yet, find our own ways to heal.

In a black and white photograph from the 1880s, a group of St. Thomas trainees in high-collared dresses, in hats, scarves, and bonnets, pose in three rows outside a brick building with long windows reaching almost to the ground. Several of the nurses hold bouquets; the skirts of those seated in front are overladen with blossoms. In the foreground, baskets spill over with more fresh blooms. In the background, slightly to the right, the blurred features of Florence Nightingale, no longer thin and peaked, but rather round and satisfied, peer out through an open window.

W.J. HERBERT

ARTS & LETTERS / RUMI PRIZE FOR POETRY

JOURNAL OF THE PLAGUE YEAR

—I saw both these stars, and I must confess… that I was apt to look upon them as the forerunners and warnings of God's judgements…—H.F. (Defoe)

1.

Buriers dumped bodies into pits after hauling
them from shut-up houses, H.F. said

but he was a saddle maker, not a naturalist
and microscopes were little known—

so why did he believe his reader needed
a meticulous description of the shrieking
that lit up houses along London's

deserted lanes? Here, azaleas riot
beside daffodils planted before the plague—

time making another accordion fold, so that Defoe
and I seem to be writing at the same time.

2.

Sometimes I picture my lungs as ruined
as the pair surgeons took from a girl
before giving her new ones.

Lend my ventilator to someone young,
my sister said, even before the dearth
forced doctors to choose from among us.

Oh, omnipotence! Did Londoners believe
the plague was punishment from a provident God?

3.

Even if I wanted to believe a *Supreme Hand*
loosed the reins of Covid's Helios, how could I?

Most New Yorkers with means
abandoned the city, as did those well-heeled
in H.F.'s time: *London was left in tears,*

he wrote, adding that most believed
the comet, appearing before the pestilence,
was a prophecy: *heavy and solemn and slow*

but severe, terrible, and frightful.

4.

No one believes the dazzling gas
and dust that swept by us last month
was any kind of semaphore from deep space.

Even its name is technological,
acronym of the craft that spotted it:

Near-Earth Object Wide-field Infrared Space
Explorer: NEOWISE.

But are we newly wise? As the virus
drives its wild chariot across the sky
inside us, we need no omen

to announce its virulent offspring
have arrived, descendants of a common
ancestor which arose 10,000 years ago

while we, in caves, shaped flints
for skinning and later set a circle
of bluestones to speak to the sun.

W.J. HERBERT

ICE STORM

If I go back again & again
to the moment when,
opening my eyes

to the farmhouse
scene on her sofa
where I lay dozing

& I look at her
lying in bed & I stop
breathing

so I'll know if she has...

*

If, in my mind,
she's still alive
& I go back again & again

& more so lately
because the flesh
of her hand

was as warm then
as mine is now, her skin
as pink & I can't sleep

if I imagine her any other way...

*

But if I go back
& her pallor is waxy,
skin cool as the linen

I wrap her in
before two men
drive to the cemetery

with her pine box in the back
of what looks like
a delivery truck,

& I watch them lift it
onto a mechanism
whose arms will lay her in earth

which seems to know it will hold her...

*

& I go back again & again
until the farmer near his
barn is barely discernible,

the cemetery's two men
becoming, not older
but more amorphous,

will my mind's
icy frame begin to glaze? —
my mother, too,

growing vague, the way
crystals freeze at the edge
of a pond until

no one can see what's beneath...

W.J. HERBERT

LIMINAL PASSAGE

Though her hospice
worker phoned to say:
She's waiting,
I knew nothing
of how she'd cling
to death's darkening
room, wedging
fingers into its cedar
paneling; knob
of its slowly-
opening exit still
nested in her palm.

                              I touched her hand
                        & it was warm, but her eyes
                           were closed, her breath
                             ragged as a cactus
                         losing paddles, that brittle
                                   dragging
                            & though, outside,
                     a hummingbird dodged spines
                             as it kissed blooms
                               in the ocotillo,
                       we were long past extracting
                               such sweetness.

W.J. HERBERT

THE BIRTH OF VENUS

*Copper-based, the blood of the ancient horseshoe crab's
descendants is used to test the purity of injectable drugs.*

1.

Born of sea-foam and desire, Hesiod said. And though
Botticelli knew what the Black Death could do to the body,

he left out the danse macabre, memento mori: her half-
shell warmed, instead, by Zephyr's winds, flesh

copious; the hint of her rounded belly
amid roses severed and blown meant to console us.

2.

Bay winds at my back, I try to imagine
where the horseshoe crab in the sheep dog's maw
has come from. Will she crush it?

After she drops the tide flat's cast-off,
I look for punctures where she'd have sunk
her teeth into the shell, but can't find any.

3.

Had she paddled out, stopping to watch it churn
in the surf before gently drawing her jaws around it?

And after seeing what she'd retrieved,
did her owner caress its delicate casing
as he came away from the water? —

sheep dog leaping in circles as, spellbound, he held
the miraculous crab before tossing it into the dunes

4.

like a brittle frisbee. The sun, by then, low in the sky.
Beach empty. In mounded sand, a sagging flag; half-
built castle, moat swamped by incoming tide

as a goddess rises, her fleshy purse embroidered
with eggs, coppery blood unblemished.

ZOE PAPPENHEIMER

ARTS & LETTERS PRIZE FOR FICTION

APPARITIONS

An hour into the trip I alternate between staring out the train window and looking at myself reflected in it. Next to me Charlie files his nails into perfect ovals and explains the benefits of bone broth. He has packed the bag at our feet with a water bottle, hand sanitizer, and cherries wrapped in a special wax cloth that he will later wash, dry, and reuse. He remembered a book for himself and a magazine for me, which I have spread on my lap like a napkin, forgotten. I lean into him, pressing my forehead against his bicep and he responds by putting his nail file away and stroking my hair from top to bottom. His own hair, normally falling past his shoulders is, pulled back into a ponytail.

It will be Charlie's first time meeting my father and my first trip home since my father was asked to take a leave of absence from the university where he's been teaching for over twenty years. A student found an old academic paper of his on patterns of speech among males and females in which my father seemed to indicate that men have more complex linguistic capacity than women. The student wrote a pithy caption and Twitter had a field day.

The college newspaper ran the first story and then the *Gazette* picked it up and of course it was all over social media by then. In private he told me the study had been a throwaway, too small to be conclusive, but he told the media something else. "I'm not apologizing for the fact that men and women are different," the paper quoted him as saying. "If men's brains process language better, it's not my fault."

❖

He told me the reporter got it all wrong, that she was against him from the start. "She was barely out of diapers," he said, "completely incompetent."

I searched for her image online, wanting to see the image of incompetence through my father's eyes. She looked just like me, as it turned out, at least in terms of age.

When the train pulls up, he is there on the platform waiting. I shoulder my backpack and Charlie follows behind with his small green wheelie. I hug my father and it is like embracing a coat on a hanger. Charlie goes in for a hug too, but my father stops him by sticking out a hand to shake and asking if his bag is so heavy, he must wheel it around like a vacuum cleaner.

Newspapers have accumulated on the front porch, which I gather under my arm, like so many baguettes. The house has never been particularly tidy, but it seems to have shifted closer to chaos, with mail and books piled up on the counters and a mountain of greasy plastic takeout containers filling the sink. There is an odor now too, the faint smell of something gone bad.

"Maggs, can you put some food out?" he yells from the stairs as he takes up our bags. The cabinets are emptier than usual and the fridge sticky, where something unidentifiable has spilled. I am slicing rectangles of cheddar onto crackers when my father comes back down and opens a can, placing a small oily fish on each cracker.

"Voila" he says.

"Dad, something doesn't smell right," I say when we are seated around the plate.

"I know, I'll lend your girlfriend some deodorant."

Charlie laughs harder than is warranted. He is a good sport, a team player. My father looks at him as if he is an idiot.

"I'm serious," I say, "What is that?"

"Can't smell," he taps the side of his nose, "good for nothing."

"Maybe something died in the walls... you wouldn't even know."

"Eat, just eat. Don't go sniffing around yet."

Charlie waits for me to start and then we begin eating. It is not a good snack, but we work at it. And as we do my father's eyes alight on Charlie's nails, the long perfect ovals of his right hand. He follows them as they reposition a sardine on a cracker. When he looks away, it is to me, eyes glowing.

"Those are some serious nails."

"Guitar." Charlie says through a bite of food, "classical." He swallows and then explains that he keeps his nails closely cropped on his left hand and grows out his right for strumming.

"Nails like that are for cocaine."

Charlie is trying to figure out if this is a joke. He hedges and tells him about his classical guitar group. Sundays, he explains, are the days they play in the park.

"I didn't touch the stuff," my father interrupts, "Cocaine, hash, LSD. I always kept to the straight and narrow. It doesn't matter though. Now you end up in the same pile of shit no matter how you live." It seems he will say more but instead he collects the plates and brings them to the sink.

He begins cleaning out the sink, depositing the takeout containers in the trash and wiping down the counters. It is often like this, my father neglecting the domestic chores until I am home, as if the sight of me reminds him someone needs taking care of.

I give Charlie a tour of the house. The downstairs takes only a minute and then we are upstairs, and I am showing him my childhood bedroom. Two sawhorses have been set up to form a makeshift workbench next to my old twin bed. On top is a disassembled AC unit, still unfixed from two summers ago, my father's toolbox left open alongside it.

I sit on the edge of the twin bed and tell Charlie that this was my parents' room before I was born. It's the nicest room in the house, with large windows overlooking the front yard, cream-colored wall-to-wall carpet, and a built-in bookshelf along one wall. It is also where my mother went into labor and where she returned from the hospital with me and the sepsis that killed her three days later.

"My father said he couldn't sleep here after that, so he's always slept in the little room down the hall. As a kid I'd talk about what happened with anyone who came by, until he told me to stop. He said, 'don't talk about death like it's a trip to the barbershop.' Ha! Well, maybe he was right. Later I found out my friends wouldn't sleep over because they thought my house was haunted."

"But it's not haunted," Charlie says, "It's where your mother lived. I'm sure you needed to talk about it, process it."

"Hmmm," I go to the bookshelf and look at the jumble of titles, *The Cat in the Hat* next to *The Color Purple*. *The Lord of the Flies* alongside *Amelia Bedelia*. It has a calming effect, like reviewing a map of the places my mind traveled as a child until I land on *Are You My Mother*, a book that troubled me even as I asked to have it read over and over. "Are you my mother?" the baby bird asks a kitten, a dog, a bulldozer. "Why does it need a mommy?" my father says I asked him, was always asking. I turn away from the book and towards Charlie whose arms open in response. Together on the twin bed, there is hardly room for the both of us and we grasp one another, to keep from falling off.

We had been living together for two months before I told my dad I was seeing someone. He was recovering from a hip replacement, and I arrived the day he was dispatched from the hospital. I drove him to pick up his prescriptions, cooked for him, and picked up the rugs when his crutches caught on them. Mostly though, we spent my visit on the couch in front of the tv. As always, he muted the commercials, saying it allowed for conversation, but we rarely spoke.

It was during one of these silent commercial breaks that I showed him pictures on my phone. Charlie and I had taken a meandering road trip centered around obscure roadside attractions. In one photo Charlie posed beside the world's largest boot, his blond hair falling neatly past his shoulders.

"So you're a lesbian now, Maggie" my father said zooming in on Charlie's face, "or is this person not a woman?"

"Ha ha," I said. "We're living together. I mean, we have been for a while now."

"So, why haven't I met him? Are you worried I'll scare him away?"

"No," I said. And then, "Would you?"

It was on that visit I saw how alone he was. No one came to visit or wish him well. It occurred to me that if I hadn't been there, he would've really struggled. Maybe he saw this too, or maybe not. When it was time for me to leave, he couldn't walk me to the train platform. He rolled down the driver's side window, a parting joke twinkling in his eye, "so long, give my regards to Charlene."

After that visit, I checked in on him over text, but it wasn't until the controversy broke over the linguistics paper, that we actually spoke again. I had already read about it on Twitter and it was like seeing one of his bad jokes fall flat, but this time in front of the whole world.

"Why would you publish something like that?" I asked.

I think maybe he had been expecting sympathy and he responded hotly, "You can't be serious. Did you read it?"

"Well, no."

"That reporter probably didn't either," he said, "she missed the nuance. I wrote that the left inferior frontal regions of the brains of female children are correlated with higher linguistic accuracy. But those studies couldn't be reproduced for adults. For adult males I found the reverse was often true."

"But the issue was the gender bias in the tests you were giving. If that's the case, wouldn't you expect bias in the results?"

"If you want to discuss this with me, read the paper."

"Ok," I said, "but if you publish something and conclude women are less smart than men, of course people are going to be pissed."

"I didn't draw that conclusion."

"But maybe you think it?"

My father was silent for so long I looked at my phone to make sure we were still connected. "Your mother was the smartest person I ever met," he said finally.

Now we swat at mosquitos as we eat dinner on the back porch. My father has made spaghetti and meatballs. Despite being a vegetarian for nearly a decade my father continues to serve me meat and I continue to pick it out. It is a war we used to fight aloud but have continued on in silence. Perhaps Charlie senses it. He asks what my father is doing during his break.

"Break? Ha! That's a word for it!"

"Well?" I say.

"I'll tell you. No, I'll read it to you." He gets up from the table and is gone for several minutes. When he comes back it is with his laptop open in front of him and before he is even back in his chair he is reading aloud from it. It is a long angry op-ed followed by another and then a third. At some point either I stop paying attention or he stops making sense. It is unclear.

I don't know how to respond when he finishes so I suggest Charlie and I do the dishes. We take our plates inside and my father continues to sit on the porch alone. When he comes in, he gestures at the drying rack where Charlie has placed the wax fabric he used for the cherries.

"I think your panties are dry, Charlie" he says, "I'm going to go split some logs."

"Oh, this?" Charlie picks it up, "Have you seen these? It's—" but my father is out the door and picking up his axe.

That night I locate a cribbage set and attempt to teach Charlie to play. The pegboard is between us on the kitchen table, illuminated by a perfect circle of light from the lamp above. It has been years since I last played and several times, we stop to look up the rules on my phone. The sound of my father snoring accompanies the slow progress of our pegs down the board. They are not even down the first stretch when I put down my cards.

"I need to figure out where that smell is coming from." I open and close drawers. I check under the sink and run a wooden spoon below the refrigerator.

"I can't even smell it, Maggs."

"How's that possible?" I open the oven and sniff. I pull out the recycling and poke around.

"I'm going to check the basement."

"Oh, come on," Charlie says, "it's almost midnight."

But then he is behind me as I open the basement door. There is no light leading down the stairs and we both hold onto the banister as we descend. At the bottom I swat the air in front of me to locate the string for the light bulb. It's been at least ten years since I've been down here and as far as I can tell, it is unchanged. There is still the rocking horse, the mop, the broken washing machine, and stacks of cardboard boxes. I look in the corners and then begin opening boxes, finding nothing but papers. I can't tell if we have gotten closer or farther away from the source of the smell. It is subtle and for a moment I consider the possibility that I have imagined it.

When I look up, Charlie is pulling my mother's white silk scarf from a box marked "Eleanor." I try to remember if I have ever told him my mother's name. It is the only box my father ever told me not to touch. Of course, as a child I went through it often, pressing her clothes to my face, trying on every item and replacing each one carefully before my father returned.

The scarf is large and square and I remember the silkiness of it against my skin. He drapes it carefully across his body and over one shoulder. His hair has come loose and falls forward obscuring half of his face. How many times did I wrap that scarf around my own body hoping to catch my mother reflected in the mirror? Charlie twirls, bright as a bride.

"Don't—" I start, stopping him mid-twirl. For a split second it is my mother who turns, the face of concern and love.

❖

On the platform, when we say our goodbyes, my father appears shrunken in the cold bright light of the day. Charlie extends his arms for an embrace and again is given my father's hand to shake. When the whoosh of air precedes the train I feel it on my face. I lean into it. Someone once said there are winners and losers in every family. I am thinking of this, of the winners and the losers as the train comes to a stop and we step in, dropping ourselves into the first vacant seats.

"Well, that was embarrassing," I say when the train has started moving. "Why did he have to read those letters? And the way he treated you!"

"You're not a reflection of him."

"I'm not sure. If we aren't formed by our parents or lack of parents, who are we?"

I expect him to answer but he doesn't. Instead he asks if my father has always been like that.

"Like what?"

"Like, not asking about you. That whole time he just talked about himself or asked me questions. Did you not notice?"

It is a strange sensation to watch scenery pass through a train window, to see everything and nothing at all. Like when there is so much sensation you feel nothing.

After a while he puts his arm around me and we are silent like that for the rest of the trip, for which I am grateful.

I sleep deeply that night. When I wake up it is with the awareness that something has shifted, like the stir of air pre-storm. I turn over in bed to face Charlie and at first, I only notice the softened jawline, the fuller lips and the narrowness of the wrist where the hand grasps the covers. A full moment passes before it registers completely that Charlie is a woman.

This woman who is both Charlie and not Charlie wakes up. She goes through the motions of an ordinary Saturday morning, making coffee and sunny side up eggs with toast. It is a peculiar sensation, the intimacy and attraction colliding with unfamiliarity. More peculiar still is how the Charlie of yesterday begins to slip away, starts to seem more like a cubist version of this woman, a contortion of the real thing, one split into angles and protrusions.

After breakfast she suggests we get out of the city and go for a hike. She makes lunches and places everything neatly into a backpack: hummus sandwiches, baby carrots, apple slices, and a thermos of ice-cold lemonade. It is early in the season to be hiking and there are patches of snow in places and not many people on the trail. As it grows steeper the trail isn't wide enough for the two of us and I follow her, alternating my gaze between the path and the bobbing of her backpack.

"It makes me mad," I say, "You asked on the train if I noticed the way my dad treats me. I almost can't handle how mad it makes me. I'm afraid of it sounding corny, but I just wish I had a father capable of expressing love or at the very least, interest. I don't think it's just me though, or at least at some point in my life I started thinking maybe it was all women. That there was something inherent in women that he rejected."

I keep talking; it is as if a lifetime of feeling has found its release. At the top, my face is wet from the exertion. Charlie draws me to her, it is a hug that is all-encompassing, and we stay like that for a long time. We stay like that until she suggests we unpack our lunches and look out at the view, at how far we have come.

THE SOL NOTES: DEAD RECKONING

I.

Plan on white picket fences. A man
to slide his slippers under your bed.
A man called Sol. White roses climbing
across black iron railings. Bunk beds.
Petite pedal pushers and onesies
baking on the clothesline. Gingerbread
baking in the oven. Love notes.

>*Hi, Mommy,*
>>*I went to the bank*
>
>*I got the lottery tickets*
>*and I went to the cleaners*
>*I was a smart little boy*
>>*Love, Sol*

Four p.m. On his way home from work, past
the Beehive bar — the Honeyhole. Bees are tired.
One beer, two. Whisky. Bees get buzzed.
Bees get loaded. What waggles out cross-eyed —
honey bee or killer bee?   Five o'clock.   Six.
Plan on fireworks. Not Fourth of July.

>*Hi, Honey,*
>*Have a good day*
>*See you to-nite*
>>*Yours forever*
>>*Sol*

Whisky-soured, *you-dumb-black-bastard*-soused,
forty-six pickled years. Plan on archives.
Tape-crossed boxes enshrouded in basements.
Christmas baubles. Treasured toys. Scraps of folded
faded paper. Wedding vows. Funeral programs.
The things you keep. The things you bury.

> *Don't worry   I'm O.K.*
> *See you soon*
> *Love, Sol*

II.

Plan for everything. Living wills, dead wills.
Buy three burial plots — for parents, Brother, me
— double-deep-down, room for (non-)future spouses.

She proclaims: *Don't bury me with Sol.*

Plan on a lifeboat without oars   incoming fog
water under the bridge, flowing backward
a lighthouse with a 25-watt bulb

You make her say it again.

III.

Take a vow and keep it unto death.
Yet how long does eternity reckon contracts?
At the crisscross of our promise and her pledge,
which obeisance should we put asunder?

Then the Sol notes are uncovered.
Joined together   *Yours forever*

IV.

When the time for white roses comes,
plan for forgiveness. The rights of the wronged,
the stings of love and honor — set these aside
if the crux of duty is a Hobson's choice

from the One who has
a plan for everything.

VERNITA HALL

Whiteout

Nothing prepares you for absolute whiteness
like a Wyoming blizzard—a bowl of cold milk
poured into the eye of a hurricane.

Inside you float alone
like tears in the mind's eye,
like every class in high school.

On the weekly bus trip of the club
you thought you'd joined,
driving into a neighborhood nobody knew

was your own where they'd privilege poor
kids of color, with a teamed cold shoulder
the snowflakes freeze you out.

Frostbitten you sit by the window
like a bird on a nest of cracked eggs.
You become that bird.

If limbo is a landscape without landmarks
perhaps this is limbo:
you and your sins alone marking time

on a clock with no hands, no face,
just that ticking tinnitus in the mind's ear.
You become that clock.

Your colored face becomes your sin.
Perhaps this is hell
and no matter how they whitewash it

maybe hell is post-racial.
But unlike a Wyoming blizzard
a world without color is

never a world all white.

JANE ZWART

TO SHUCK MIRACLES

There is another world, but
the surrealist guesses that
it is inside this one.

We must want it to be true.
Somewhere a man pulls
the innards from every outlet

in his house. In the empty
Raco boxes, he contrives
tiny rooms. One is a study.

An anthill of tobacco
spills from a pipe
into a red melamine bowl.

There is, inside this world,
another. My student writes
I drive a purple Equinox!

and I pour the sentence
out. I evict her Chevrolet.
Instead, let her thread

the mountain pass cleft,
perfect, between dark
and day, in a violet chariot,

in chiaroscuro. So strong
is the urge to shuck
miracles that we run

thumbnails through the seams
of maples' samaras to loose
their spring-loaded tongues.

JANE ZWART

CERTAIN MAPLES

At ten I considered a punch of Fresca
and rainbow sherbet an aperitif, the mixed
drink of sophisticates. I had never seen
a rosette pat of butter or swans hewn
from blocks of ice.
               Anyway, certain
maples — the young ones on mulch islands
in genteel parking lots, still pale green
and lemon in the places frost finds last

but mostly impossibly salmon — they put me
in the mind of those cloudy suspensions
served at nubile cousins' showers.

It is not that I want to color leaves thirsty
for light with the inorganic Pantone
of pastels and confections. I do not want
to praise the vivid tree by comparison
with articial things. But how else to say this?

I could drink these maples like a punch:
citrus-flavored submersibles and tropical froth,
carcinogenic sweeteners, milky soda, and all.

RAPHAEL RAE

INTRODUCTION TO SAFECRACKING FOR TRANSSEXUALS

Strong inside me, as a crashing wave or the lunar force that tugs its salted punch ashore, is the sense that of course I will keep myself safe. Who will, after all, if I don't? Who will bury me in the panic room, who will go for the defensive chef's knife, go for the jugular, aim a knee to the balls or an elbow to the diaphragm or — This is how safe plays out in my head, a dramatic choreographing, visceral violence. Since I was small, I've obsessively, regularly conjured elaborate fantasies of threats to my body from another body, and thought my way through how I would run and hide or, if it came down to that, how I would fight. What better way to self-soothe than to draw up anxious images of an armed intruder breaking into my home, and directing my imaginary meat and muscles into kicking the backs of his knees, into thrusting my hard forehead against the complex bird's nest of his nose, blurting a spray of his blood across my face? Yes, I will keep myself safe. I would never do the opposite. Always, I think this, until the moment it ceases to be true.

Until, in my small-child form, I decide to enter the playground where a boy who hates me and his posse of backup swing, and I spit on the boy when he tells me to go, so they follow us into the adjacent woods, looming, and now their swinging means swinging a threatening pipe. Until in high school I bike down fully unlit streets to reach a friend's party, almost hit by multiple cars, eyes capturing images — or an absence thereof — that will lead to years of nightmares where I'm carried along by the congress of my muscles and a machine in perfect black, awash on the tides of night. Until, at eighteen, I follow a boy I met on the train into an abandoned apartment to smoke together. Until, at nineteen, I nearly pass out in the jacuzzi tub embedded in the floor of mine and my girlfriend's Honeymoon Suite from the combination of the heat, the added bubble bath's oxygen-hunger — bubbles piling higher than my head — and the wine in my hand and in my blood. Until, twenty-four, drunk on ciders from the bar slash pinball arcade slash laundromat where we throw my coworker's going-away party, I climb into a car with an equally drunk coworker wobbly behind the wheel. Until, at four a.m. of my twenty-seventh birthday, I snort a stranger's coke off a key despite knowing that New York's supply has been tainted with fentanyl lately. Until, twenty-five, although I meet Yousef for the first time, after Tinder exchanges, in the publicity of a coffee shop, I decide then and there to trail them home for them to happily hurt me, and I don't tell anybody where I'm going or with whom.

I confess to them later this last absence of precaution, and they're upset to hear it, tell me that it was stupid and that I should never do it again; I know this, but an unshakeable trust in them at hearing them first speak burbled up in me like a mineral spring, healing, and I wasn't wrong. In none of the above situations did my stupidity lead me to harm; I have not consistently kept myself safe, but often, dumb luck has. Enforcing in my brain a trauma-born understanding of myself as powerless, weak against the universe's whims, tossed about in its gale.

Camping, Kiya and I stumble upon a large, rusting safe thrown out by the side of the road, hidden down a dusty hill, amongst Jack's-beanstalk-tall weeds. Two holes have been bored through the side, and any erstwhile valuable contents are long-gone. Like a vampire's victim: punctured at the neck and drained. Kiya's hair blonder in the wild sun and mine redder, almost bloody, we pose for one another's phone cameras atop the boxy, hollowed corpse, stretched seductively, fingers on the dial, pretending to crack the combination like a shortcut hasn't been drilled through the metal off-screen. Of course, to properly crack a safe, you must press your ear to its chest, listening with a high degree of sensitivity. It's not as simple or as dumb-luck-driven as cracking a wishbone in half. To be able to enter a safe, you must be open to hearing what the safe has to say about itself, and the same is true of safety. Entering safety's embrace and reaping its riches requires a receptiveness, a tuning-in.

What else cracks, besides safes and bones? Trust; codes; knuckles; a chrysalis eventually; a door slivering ajar in offering of a new room in which to reside; a tough nut; Yousef's palm lovingly and hotly across my face or ass; a china willow-print coaster when I lift my coffee mug and the two stick together for a long moment before the blue-and-white circle falls to the ground, and then to pieces; the medically transitioning transmasculine voice. Cracking and holding/hiding are braided together. A crack in the sidewalk is a place for weeds to grow; a crack in the floorboards is an opportunity for something small to disappear. Step on the cracks and you'll break your mother's back—laughing back at the whim-rich universe: with the power of superstition on my side, I'm in control now! I say who hurts! What breaks. All decided by where I land, and I decide where I land: no roll of the dice marionettes my legs, with their bones that have sprained but never broken.

When my voice first begins cracking, I am, unusually, in church, visiting my parents in Philadelphia for the weekend. One sunlit-through-stained-glass moment I can sing the hymns passably, and then, as I lurch closer to passing, I cannot. I squeak and creak. At this point, I've been injecting testosterone weekly for about four months. My face, chest, and back are a parade of blood-and-pus-flushed zits, and my mustache and thigh hair have steadily darkened and grown. I swear my neck has gotten too thick for me to easily button the top buttons of my shirts, and my libido has soared out of control, slipping the bonds of gravity to punch the face of

God. And back in New York after my visit, I find I can no longer mimic the high meows of one of my catsitting clients—I try to sing her sweet cries back to her, in this poorly illuminated wealth-strewn mansion of an Upper West Side apartment, and nothing leaves my throat but air. I have been cut off from, kicked out of, that octave. Like the dropped coaster, my voice's highness is now broken, unusable; unlike that, there's no amount of gluing that might put it back together again. This is a real Humpty-Dumpty of a situation.

Safe is not something I often feel, despite my certainty that I will protect myself. It's as rare as me entering a church. As rare as I typically cook my steaks before tearing them to pieces with hands and teeth. Typically, I am looking over my shoulder; by now, I've turned a million wives to a million pillars of salt. My muscles are tensed, my heart beats hard, and I am prepared, perpetually, to run and hide. This is why, under harsh interrogation room light, I am shitty at self-preservation. If everything looks dangerous, how can you spot the real danger? And after years of frustrated attempts to pick out the real danger like noting where Waldo's at or discerning the snoozing polar bear in the middle of a blizzard, how can you find it in you to keep, reliably, trying? My new therapist asks me to name times in which I've felt safe, and after a pause long as a train that blocks a pursuant car inconveniently in the middle of an action-movie chase, I tell him that I felt safe with Yousef. And that now what I fear more than anything else is never again finding that total absence of fear.

From the moment we laid our bags down in the honeymoon suite at the Dominican Republic Hard Rock Café, where I would almost pass out in the in-floor jacuzzi, my girlfriend fell ill. Retired to bed, sluggish with something fluish, and stayed there for the remainder of the week, leaving me to my own devices. Mornings I spent out on the balcony in weak gray sun, rereading my way through A Series of Unfortunate Events, the epitome of treatises on eternal unsafety. By day, I wandered out to swim in one of the resort's dozen pools, or further, to the beach. It was January, and while the weather mostly reflected our proximity to the equator, the air by the sea still chilled come afternoon, stiffly ripply with salinated breeze.

Often, it was just me out there, on a chair with my towel and my book. Once, just me and an unknown woman, the two of us a couple arm's lengths apart as we forged forward into the surf. As each wave reared up equinely on its hind legs to crack wet hooves against our bodies, I'd turn my back, welcoming the hard contact with my spine. Until finally one wave smacked me too hard and I fell forward, treated to a snoutful of saltwater and who knows what accompanying microscopic creatures up my nose too. The woman came close to check if I was fine, and told me, "You should face the waves. Where I come from, in Brazil, we say to never turn your back on the ocean."

But out of her sight, I continued to turn my back on the ocean, to risk my face being mashed into the silt, salt and bacteria invited to invade my nasal passages. Too frightening for me was the prospect of facing the crash of waves with my chin jutted and eyes peeled. To see the danger and say, "Come and get me."

The best way to stay safe from a vampire is to turn your back on the world, remaining within your home, living alone, and offering no invitations. To socially isolate yourself, becoming a hermit, is to practically surround your castle with a moat of holy water, to station archers with garlic-seasoned arrows notched and ready at the slits in your apartment's edifice, narrow and lovely like a purring cat's eyes. All it takes is unwillingness to trust, to open up, to extend a hand. Laying down the welcome mat is lying down in your own grave.

Okay, so most of us don't have slits in our outer walls like that, those medieval pores, but there are often cracks in the ceiling into which we divine shapes like into clouds in the sky or tea leaves in porcelain cups. The shapes are leporine, if we're Madeline, our appendices stolen away from us in dead of night. What kind of surgery would it take for those cracks to grow antlers, becoming jackelopes, a sutured fiction existent only in posed death? A posed implication of an otherworldly beauty that could be, but was not born? Will top surgery do this to me, I ask in the time leading up to my remodeling. Will it make me see myths? Take my tits and leave me a jackelope god splayed above my hospital bed; we are a new kind of manmade (made-man) thing in each other's eyes.

After my appendectomy at nineteen, still rising to the surface of my consciousness, higher than the clouds (and my future libido) on painkillers, I did not see rabbits, but I still had massive, omniscient creatures on the mind, urgently telling Melanie, who stood at my bedside, "Mount Olympus was the original Big Brother," before I lapsed back into sleep. Body altered by human hands, stirring in my brain was the potential smallness of gods, surveilled by humankind, which had grown out of control through technology. Gods locked away in the safes of our televisions—or our proto-televisions: our folk-telling mouths.

Does God place a roving eye to the rabbit cracks in our ceilings to see us, the way we might spy through wounds in a wall or door? In Patricia Highsmith's novel *The Price of Salt*, unsafety comes from being spied upon. Private romance is transformed into custody battle paydirt through the application of listening devices, and the very first listening device—we learn long after it's made its entrance, performance, and bow—is a spike hammered through the lovers'—Therese and Carole's—hotel room wall. Crude and artless. Immediately, I think of a vampire, staked through the heart. All the (after)life gone from it in one thrust, corpse crumbling to dust. To record is to intrude is to disintegrate. To salt the slug of clandestine love. Turn it into poison; turn it into evidence of deviance, unfitness. Not slotting in, a key in the wrong lock, no legitimate entryway into the safe, into safety.

An over-attachment to the boundaries of home might keep us safe from vampires, but it can keep vampires safe as well. Dracula never goes anywhere without the security blanket of a coffin full of his own grave's dirt. Vampire and would-be victim: mirror images when outfitted in their chosen, home-y armor; who says vampires cast no reflection? Unless they are themselves the reflection, the ephemeral, the repeating, the voice on skipping-disk, while victims are the original bodies. The ones casting, as well as directing, movement.

"Mushrooms move the ground slightly as they grow," Anna Lowenhaupt Tsing writes in *The Mushroom at the End of the World*. ". . . I think of sensing a heave, an effect like the inhalation of breath in the chest. The heave is easy to imagine as the breath of the mushroom. There may be a crack, as if the mushroom's breath escaped." What escaped when my voice cracked, heaving from my chest, up my throat, between my lips? What moved me with its growth? Letting go of ghosts, of fears. My innards serving as a hothouse for bravery.

Now seeking my world to crack open like an oyster. Or how a bridge cracks down the middle in a disaster movie and everybody spills into the sea. Dreamy: spilling into the sea, the opposite of turning my back on her ebb and flow. Caught in disaster, like Dorothy in the twister, carried to technicolor and heroism without lifting a finger — yet every finger and other bones lifted. If only things were larger for me, brighter for me. If only a brick road, glowing gold, to see by. A field of poppies to dream by. A horse of Joseph's-coat's colors to ride astride. Seeking, through personal ads on a dating app, modern newsprint. Through my opened kitchen window and onto the fire escape. Through my sternum and out my spine in a clean line. Should I seek through binoculars, get into birding? Into searching for life? Or the same but downward: searching for mushrooms, for the openings where their breath has left?

In the wake of my top surgery, my blood pressure surges too high, and I'm kept in my surgical bed in the office for four long hours as my roommate and a nurse who bears my deadname sit beside me, chatting and feeding me fluorescently pink Gatorade, the nurse periodically accompanying me to the bathroom to see if I can pee, pumped full enough of fluid (I never do successfully urinate in that office, but finally lie to her and say that I have, desperate to end the repeated trips like a record skipping). No jackelope appears in the ceiling smooth as ice freshly Zamboni-ed, but my Deadname Nurse describes to us the house she and her husband recently bought, which came with one room entirely pink. Walls pink, ceiling pink, hardwood floors stained pink. A Barbie Dreamhouse, or an intestinal paradise. I'm jealous of this conjured vision, having come so far from the little boygirl who pretended to loathe the color pink, who made a big show of ducking and hiding from Barbies, desperate to assert an ungirlness, ashamed of their actual love of these things, unable yet to identify this as a fear of being effeminate, faggy. The gendered world not yet cracked open to that possibility, that femininity could actually mark me as a deviant. Deadname Nurse says that she and her husband painted over all of the pink; I internally seethe.

In the waiting room for my neurologist, at age twenty-one, an age at which I assumed I would die soon, I met a man who told me that I reminded him of the singer P!nk. My short, bleached hair was the obvious point of connection; if anything else cemented the similarity for him, he didn't share. He told me that she was his favorite artist. "My wife knows that when the P!nk records are on, not to bother me. That's my P!nk time." Soon, he would fly to Germany to see her in concert.

I said, "That's a long way to go," and he told me, "Maybe, but life is too short not to."

When I laid down the welcome mat for Sam, two months before my top surgery, I was safe about it, kept my promise to Yousef that I would not repeat following a stranger home with no one knowing my destination. We met in Maria Hernandez Park, spreading like a picnic blanket a green flannel sheet on which to sprawl, both wrapped in leather jackets, and a drag show pulsing loudly nearby. I sought brighter colors in my world through a very horny personal ad, and now here was a real horny boy before me. Our bodies grew closer as the sky grew darker. When he asked me, "So, uh, do you want to make out?" with a squirm in his mouth, I acquiesced easily, sinking into him, siren-songed, dusk and chill draping over us as we became the sole figures still lounging in the grass, others dispersing, drag show long over, our mutually cracked voices silenced, mouths distracted. And I did not go home with him that night, nor he with me. There would be other nights.

Belated for my birthday, Sam gifts me a knife that is a necklace that is a cat wearing a bow-tie. Heavy, brass, blade tucked into graceful body, ready to spring. He wants me to have a weapon; he wants me to be safe; instead, not expecting genuine sharpness, utility, protection, I immediately slice my thumb on the knife's point, blood weeping copiously down the boulder of my hand. Sakiya asks me over Facebook Messenger if I paid him for the gift—even a penny, just a token. She explains, "If you get a knife as a gift and don't pay for it, then at best the knife will cut you and at worst it will cut your relationship." A pause in our digital communication during which I contemplate whether or not to Venmo my boyfriend a single ceremonial cent, and then Kiya's decree, handed down from Ozarks family superstition: "It already cut you, so your relationship is safe."

My own blood on my hands: the inverse and—by the logic that the exception proves the rule—the ceremonial seal of keeping myself safe. For months after Yousef's twenty-fifth birthday, my right elbow ached to bear weight, from how I banged myself up walking to their apartment, carrying with me the painting I made for them of a scene from their favorite *Simpsons* episode. A trip on the sidewalk so slapstick-dramatic that two men who witnessed it from over a block away asked if I was okay when we finally crossed paths. Robin's-breast-red oozed from both palms; my skin burned like a blush, or bush—something that tells truth, despite my lying, "Yes."

For the one-year anniversary of my decision not to kill myself, Melanie and I walked into town to attend church, celebrating what I chose to call my rebirthday, a day that was celebrated the first time around with my first-ever ice cream sundae from the Friendly's across from our apartment, which sat right next to the cemetery in a bit of poetic heavyhandedness. On the way to church, I drink my coffee from a mug, incongruously domestic amidst the wide white sidewalks and institutional buildings of the UMass Amherst campus through which we cut. Upon swigging the last drop, I plop the mug into the navy pleather purse that was temporarily confiscated from me—full of makeup—when I checked myself into the mental hospital one year ago. I must plop with too much force, because the mug's handle amputates itself, and the next time I reach into my bag's oceanic depths, I slice open my palm on jagged ceramic. What the psychiatric nurses feared I might do by splintering my cosmetics' plastic cases to shards has finally come to pass, but through happy accident rather than desperation to feel, and it is happy; I smile in wonder at the scarlet outpouring. Blood highlights every legible line in my palm, head and heart and life, and without thinking, I raise my hand and smear more blood onto my forehead, like ashes from a religion I do not practice. Anointing myself. Making-sacred.

On my way to church: a mug cracks. In church: my voice cracks. Who can help but see the obvious, that cracking is holy? When we crack under the pressure, when we crack the puzzle, when we crack a joke—we get closer to God. God is in the openings, in the mouseholes, in the fence-breaches and gaps between teeth, and in the sharpness of action with which these things come into being.

Sam's roommate on the other side of his bedroom wall has an Alexa. She loves to talk to the fucking Alexa. The stake hammered in through the wallpaper. The eye searching through the ceiling cracks. Once, I catsat for a heterosexual couple with an Alexa controlling the lights in their basement, and the wife explained to me, "Alexa only listens to my husband's voice, not mine. I tell her, Alexa lights on, and she ignores me," and I think dear god please throw this misogynist baby out with its surveillance state bathwater, but for all I know this woman is still, years later, living with a watchful WiFi-enabled god and an inability to turn on the lights. The reason the Ancient Romans believed that breaking a mirror would bring seven years of bad luck was that mirrors were windows the gods used to spy on your soul, and it was disrespectful to interfere with their prying—the reverse of my drug-hazy Mount Olympus = Big Brother equation. We were the original Big Brother. Seven years was the length of time it took to grow a whole new soul.

Six years ago, I read online that a mirror could be cut cleanly with scissors if you held it underwater, so I submerged my full-length mirror in the bathtub, positioned it between the scissors' silver legs, and clamped, and *crack*. The whole thing splintered, leaving me with a pile of jagged icicles of Alexa-ish Window Into My Soul, of Vampire Detection Tool, of bad fucking luck. I took a large triangular chunk of glass and glued it to my final for my art class, a heavy wooden plank I'd painted all over with images of myself in red underwear, my duplicate heads covered up by the very real electrodes I'd peeled off my hospital-released body days before.

Melanie once gifted me a blue-and-white figurine of a saint with a bird for a head, its wings outstretched and beak like a poised knife. Dried glue wends an ochre path down the figure's center, tracing the journey a mortician's scalpel would take in the service of peeling back the meat of the ribcage and onward, accessing the holy organs to turn them into keepsakes. This is how I understand my top surgery scars—simply glue, from how I was shattered and made into something brand new. Jackeloped. Eloped with myself. When I first took off my compression vest and saw my new flat chest in the mirror, I said, "Oh, there you are." Imagine I say this thirteen times and conjure myself like Bloody Mary, reach through the watery reflective surface to take my hand and run to home base, to safe. To you-can't-tag-me-out.

When speaking to an Alexa, remember *The Price of Salt*. To record is to intrude is to disintegrate. She is always keeping a record. Even if she will not listen to your voice in the sense of obeying and turning on the lights, she is holding your voice captive, her prize possession, like Ursula the seawitch giving out legs left and right. Emotion becomes evidence.

Data pointing to deviance. I wonder if the Alexa can hear as Sam fucks me on the other side of the wall. Deviants. Defiant. Two boys shattered and soldered from pristine pink beginnings, who both love to stand with our backs to the ocean. There even sits, on his bicep, a Friday the 13th flash tattoo that the artist called a shatter but Sam called a crack, lines radiating from a central point of breakage.

While the crack was penned into his skin, I received a thick-lined rose on my lower left arm from a trans man in a Gatorade-pink plastic apron.

Oh there you are oh there you are oh there you are oh there you are oh there you are oh there you are oh there you are oh there you are oh there you are oh there you are oh there you are oh there you are oh there you are.

Reading poetry by the open kitchen window, I find myself ensnared in vivid thoughts of unpeeling my knife from its feline form and re-slicing along the rope of my chest scars, textured as they are like vinyl car interior. Deface the automobile of me. Classic country song jilted ex behavior, where I am my own spurned lover. Last night, I bled on camera for Sam, for a class project, transforming life into art if nothing else, sitting on his flowery bed and pulling my syringe from my muscle and leaving behind a glorious red river, dark and bright by turns. How startled I was by the depths of my recorded voice, upon reviewing the footage, when I laughed and asked for paper towels, having slapped a lime-green star-print bandage over the exit wound and left to deal with an outsized stoplight smear along my hairy thigh. For a moment, hearing myself (head cut off by the frame's edges, voice-source anonymized through the magic of boundary), I thought a third person had entered the room. Maybe Bloody Mary; maybe P!nk; maybe Dracula or God. Of course, there is a third body: the camera, that stake through the fourth wall, capturing.

My friend Sarah told me that she's always loved my voice, even before she knew me well, and then, ironic sentiment braiding in, added that she could not remember that high voice she first loved; it had been so thoroughly erased by this new low register, what she affectionately, from her own gay social positioning, called "fag voice." She added, to be clear, "That's the medical term."

I must address the elephant in the room. That which I have talked about freely but which serves as a glaring omission in my list of instances in which I did not keep myself safe. For what greater swim through uncharted, drag-on-strewn waters have I taken than choosing to transition? Transitioning specifically into fag-voiced effeminacy. Into a form that causes a man on the subway platform to point at me and loudly proclaim, "What is that?" And when I say "elephant," I really do stand by my idiom, stroking its trunk and feeding it peanuts, because this is something larger and livelier than those stupid split-second choices that haunt me eternally with nagging what-ifs, visions of alternate timelines spinning off, my body in unlucky-cat-black clothes and a coffin. This is an intelligent, emotional, King Kong of a being, this choice. This journey. Skipping down this yellow brick road, gazing down the double barrel of violent bigotry and mind-twisting bureaucracy that I could have sidestepped if I'd simply decided to playact cis womanhood to the pink-stained grave, it's easy to say, "That's a long way to go."

Every day, it's easier to say back, "Maybe, but life is too short not to."

Every day, it's easier to see the danger and say, "Come get me."

When I visited the courthouse to turn over my petition for a name change, the security guard positioned by the metal detectors and X-Ray machines confiscated the weapon on my keys: thick purple plastic molded into the shape of a pitbull's face, the eyes holes through which to put my fingers and the ears tall and sharp, perfect for stabbing an assailant. I'd been carrying around some variation on this device since I was assaulted while running by the river when I was seventeen, and it had become such an extension of me that it never would have occurred to me to leave the pitbull at home, even though I knew what the guard explained: "This is an illegal weapon in the city of New York." This is why Sam chose to gift me a weapon, this giving up I had to do. This overt act of trading, unwillingly, a piece of my safety, for a piece of legitimacy as a trans person. I wanted my weapon. I wanted my name more; but whether I was ready to give up one for the other is not something that anyone asked me. The decision was taken out of my hands, and so was my stabby companion. All part of the process — which mirrors Carole and Therese's intimacy and care for one another transforming into courtroom evidence — of my intimacy with and care for myself transforming into something that the state can choose or choose not to legitimate. Because it is an act of intimacy and care, to name myself the right thing. To become Raphael is to become a sacred figure and a sword-bearer and a man and a me.

To be able to enter a safe, you must be open to hearing what the safe has to say about itself. To be able to enter your gender, you must be open to hearing what your self has to say about itself. Inside: riches. Inside: sex. Inside: love. Inside: beautiful bloody art. Inside: the chrysalis cracks down the middle, and out springs out a sacred figure with a bird for a head and visible glue and maybe jackelope antlers rising high like TV antennae and maybe vampire fangs implying a sentimental attachment to the rich earth of home, and to this reflection, disco-ball-sparkling, dissolving into the boundaries of my flesh, I say, oh there you are oh there you are oh there you are, oh there — and let the ocean interrupt me as it smacks me full in the face, full of salt and life, my eyes open wide to its sting, its illumination of new worlds and realms of being.

PROLOGUE #9

What does your body remember?

If the beginning must begin
the body must be considered.

my birth
mother's blood
is smoke stirring
in the forest
of my forgetting

my birth
mother's body
is a leash my memory
bites, tugs toward barking
— *betrayal betrayal*

She is alive. She lives in North Mpls. We met.
I was born at Saint James Hospital, 6:22 p.m.

                    But in my childhood dreams
The beginning was sunlight arresting the wind.

What mother? What mother.

It was simple. Instead of birth, I lay alive
without a body beneath a canopy of pine
growing gold toward the sky.

If I was anyone's son,
it was only of sound; water returning to water,
the sap beetle's soft chew — *think of that!* To be

mothered by the music
of hunger, by the chuckle of dried pine, crisp
copper needles laughing loudly against the land.
Listen —

If I was anyone's son,
it was only of what nouns the forest ripened
with wind: fruit-wood, cypress, boy mothered
by the swinging white moss, mothered by red
clay, glossed maroon mud animated by rain.

How pretty. How perfect.

How often is memory
a mirror reflecting only
what won't shatter it?

Silly child. To read
foster-care then conjure *forest.*
To read *biological* then dream
the earth your lucent-green womb.

If ever a mother she was
the night's scintillant moon — a pocked single
parent sickled by distance. For each dark mile
I dreamt a new not-mother:

Mother made of cricket song. Mother made
of buzzing city wires. Of flashing metal birds
cleaving thin gray clouds, of midnight's silver
mist. Each imagined mother a bright, brief
ghost. Ghosts all missing by morning.

ERIN CARLYLE

ARE WE REALLY LIVING IN A SIMULATION?

In the future a computer on the moon runs
      the simulation: me as a child barefoot
           in the woods, and my momma in her blue

overcoat cooking ham and beans,
      fried cornbread, and then calling for me
           to come in. Over and over, it repeats my daddy

opening the door of his semi — exhausted
      from his haul. He steps down careful
           not to fall, and he never

falls. It replays my daddy calling the police
      on a man in a Buick who stopped me and tried
           to get me in his car, and it repeats

me running fast past the little green
      store and my best friend's house all the way home.
           This computer changes the mass

of the moon, and its job. It'll learn,
      but it's not the same as a lesson
           learned. I don't know if there are people

in this future who smudge
      their foreheads with ash, or people who
           deny themselves food in repentance

except a little bread and water. This is just data
        not ritual: me driving my rental car
                to the funeral home and then claiming

daddy's remains, and me walking
        through the airport carrying his urn
                in a box. The computer plays

moments, but it can't analyze them not even
        those moments when my daddy grew stiller
                and stiller. He'll just go and then begin again.

MARCUS CAFAGNA

FRIENDLY FIRE

1.

I can't recall which cousin swore Aldo's knees had locked
in a nervous shake from the combat he'd seen. His knees would
pump, all ways, as he shifted the weight in his chair,
rocking himself as if he was back to being the age of nine.
His hands trembled as he appeared to move toward
somewhere safer in his head. I never dared to ask
why his face was cast in permanent five o'clock shadow
like a man who needed a shave. I wondered if it was true
that a hand grenade burn he suffered from an exploded
pineapple, olive-drab, dropped accidentally by a comrade
clearing the beaches of landmines before a botched
invasion of the Italian coast in October of 1943,
had instead blown up in poor Aldo's face.

2.

Raised with the terror of Blackshirts breaking in
to arrest and deport his father for helping Jewish friends
escape Italy, Aldo lived, after this,
in Michigan. There, he wrote aspirin commercials
for Bayer and a war novel no one would ever read.
When it came his time to fight, his infantry division had landed,
only to be pinned by gunfire, in Naples—his place of birth.
How he must have felt to stand—a Yankee GI
on the volcanic soil of ash deposits after the fall
of El Duce. He had then to live his life in the afterglow

of surviving a frag grenade blast, close range.
He had then to avoid his mother and sisters at times,
preferring to stay hidden in a cloud of Lucky Strikes.

3.

I never knew what to say at family gatherings
as I sat, at dinner, across the table from him—
when his knees would start to knock, when he couldn't
seem to sit still. He was ever on high alert,
expecting radio-guided bombs to burst
any minute over grayed skies of Detroit.
Always, he smiled the bull-faced smile
of the defeated, preparing himself
for the worst—for some detonation of gunpowder
to release into our air, knocking just him out.
He would be revealed to us then the young soldier
he was when the southern region of his face
had been set on fire—doused hot silver, afterbirth.

MARCUS CAFAGNA

LOST THE SIGNAL

Like someone first learning to speak,
his words come out halting and few.
Not so long ago, he could outtalk us all,
before the chemo left my father's memory
stuck. I think he still knows who I am,
because he tells me to go home,
though my plane just landed. But I'm not sure
I know him since the cancer fenced
him to a hospice bed—his body
so shrunken, his shock of hair
turned silver, the veins in his arms
bulged blue against his crepe paper skin.
As I blather on about nothing,
he shifts his gaze from the TV to eye me
through a pair of tortoise-shell rims,
touches a bony index finger
to his temple and says, *Lost the signal.*
I shrug, not knowing what the hell
he means. Not taking his eyes off mine,
he points his finger again, this time
at his forehead, and repeats the words,
Lost the signal, like someone losing
his mind. He rolls those dark eyes
toward the window, where my stepmother
has hung a blue stained-glass bird,
its ruby wings spread in perpetual flight.
Instead of us speaking, he wants

to share this moment of his dying, this
silence between father and son, where words
hold no meaning. Later, here in the kitchen,
when I tell Beth how he touched
his head and told me he lost the signal,
she says, without emotion or pause,
Yeah, that's what he says if the batteries
in his hearing aid are running low.

KATHRYN HARGETT-HSU

Petition for Naturalization

ALWAYS GIVE YOUR ALIEN REGISTRATION NUMBER WHEN COMMUNICATING WITH THIS SERVICE

ALWAYS the immigration officer's confident pen,
a black blister, to GIVE us a new body.

Three hundred petitions:
    yellow to medium brown to medium
    Mongoloid to medium fair to medium
    white to medium:

        YOUR revision logged in a wide folder
        of ALIENs lapping at the harbor.

From 1882-1965, America federally slammed its door
on Chinese immigrants' toes.
Weeks confined to isolation wards.
Their names skewered on REGISTRATION forms
    (or returned to the wine-dark sea).

        It is impossible to know the NUMBER of Chinese laborers
        maimed in pursuit of the ocean.
            (That is: the Central Pacific Railroad kept no
        record of their deaths.)

        WHEN nineteen Chinese were lynched
        on a single night in 1871, a fair man
        cut off a medium man's finger in pursuit of a ring.

1970s: first Chinese restaurant in North Alabama.
My grandparents spoke little English.
      The fluent daughter was tasked
      with COMMUNICATING WITH the fair customers.
Nonthreatening vocabulary & nonthreatening chop suey smiles.

When the general died of tuberculosis,
    four generations were quarantined in THIS small house.
      The smallest of them slept in drawers.

Some labored in the SERVICE of nationhood.
Some died before they could return.

When the Tennessee River flooded,
    they collected the exiled carp no fair people
    would harvest.

(I?)   the ungrateful progeny go for the eyes.

ORIGINAL
(To be retained
by Clerk of Court)

UNITED STATES DEPARTMENT OF JUSTICE
Immigration and Naturalization Service

UNITED STATES OF AMERICA

PETITION FOR NATURALIZATION

No. _13,024_
A.R. No. A35 135 165

To the Honorable
The ___District___ Court for the ___United States___ at ___Birmingham, Alabama___

This petition for naturalization, hereby made and filed under section ___316(a)___
Immigration and Nationality Act, respectfully shows:

(1)

Hang an American flag from your window.

TRUE & CORRECT, the angel will pass over you.

(2)

In my classroom, the PRESENT PLACE OF fair:

Blond hair braided with dandelions.
Lunchables & crustless sandwiches & mini muffins.

My fair classmate trying my own afternoon snack,
then retching nothing on the floor.

After school,

I lit a candle in my bathroom
& cast a spell for green eyes.

I stared at my reflection, willing flora
to take RESIDENCE
in dirt iris.

(3)

Fair people do not own nature stories.

Who said they could take it from us?

We were all BORN IN the trees,
        slept in the canopy before we had language
            to describe it.

            Write about flowers.

            Bloody your hands with a blueberry bush.

(4)

I REQUEST THAT MY NAME
    BE CHANGED TO   dirt eye.

(5)

Humid summers in unceded land.
Two radio stations.

        Pawpaw could still drive.

In the back seat, I drank fresh orange juice
with my medium sister.

        Around us,

    wide acres of unceded lumber,
    guinea fowl chasing cars down dirt roads.

The hawks HAVE NOT ABANDONED
    SUCH RESIDENCE of their inheritance.

We invade.

(6)

Nana dotting Country Lily 01 foundation on my cheeks,
smearing it into fair ash on my medium face.

Our difference cast in no shadow
         & CONTINUOUSLY IN THE STATE.

(7)

How she once touched the UNION of my eyelids
& wondered aloud,   *Where's the crease?*

(8)

After a few generations, you, too, can become fair,
if blended with fair people.

    Trade bok choy for green peas
    & oyster sauce for ketchup.

        It comes not IMMEDIATELY UPON TERMINATION
        but like a fissure in plaster,

            the tectonic plates
            BY TREATY OR STATUTE

        pulling apart the ground.

Form N-405 (Rev. 11-27-78)N

(9)

Assimilation is a bureaucratic practice.

Complexion is an OTHER THAN HONORABLE euphemism,
which can be scratched out
　　　in black pen, corrected.

Fair, medium, dark.

　　That is: you are between states.

　　That is: subject or accomplice.

　　　I cross the unceded stream again & again.

　　　　Medium daughters of fair father,
　　　　fair daughters of medium mother—

　　I HAVE NEVER BEEN SEPARATED FROM
　　　　this riverbed, that bisection AGGREGATING
　　　　　the conditions of medium containment.

　　That is: do what you're told.

　　That is: fair violence & SERVICE TERMINATED.

(10)

　　A pen can waterboard or LAWFULLY ADMIT.

The wisdom, once:

> to be counted is to be subject
> > to the (neo)colonial enterprise.

> > So: decategorize.

> > So: become unmeasurable.

> REFUSE TO WEAR THE UNIFORM of empire.

(11)

(12)
But the instructions are unclear.
> > For so long
> I BELIEVED IN,
> > ADVOCATED,
> ENGAGED IN
> > my own vanishing.

I compass my yearning
                    out the window,
                            to the oak trees,

        thinking of Mitsuye Yamada.
                How invisibility is an unnatural disaster.

                To become uncountable,
                                        debureaucratic,
                without disappearing altogether,

                        is an impossible proposition.

(13)
        In the nineteenth and twentieth centuries,

        the United States did not consider Chinese women
                GOOD MORAL CHARACTER, slits

                        DISPOSED TO THE GOOD ORDER
                of an infiltrating snake.

                        Inscribed into law:

                        Medium & lewd & immoral.
                        Medium & where is your decency?

            In 1875,
        Ulysses S. Grant invited Congress to consider

"perhaps no less an evil—the importation of Chinese
women, but few of whom are brought to our shores
to pursue honorable or useful occupations."

Inscribed into the archive:

Medium deviant.
Medium & venomous to the national bloodstream.

Sign along the dotted line:

I will not poison you.

(FULL NAME, WITHOUT ABBREVIATION.)

(14)

One summer I followed my fair father & his fair cousin
to shoot Coke cans in the woods.

When it was my turn to shoot,

my father showed me safety from reload,
how to stand
so the recoil wouldn't shove me down.
I took WITHOUT QUALIFICATION
THE OATH of a medium finger
against the trigger.

I lowered the target between the sights;
inhaled;
squeezed;

& missed the can completely.
The fair men expected it of me.

For the rest of the afternoon,
I was EXEMPTED THEREFROM conducting injury
with my own paws.

Instead, I accompliced.

I loaded .22 bullets into magazines
& watched the fair men use the machine,

which breathed,
which could PERFORM NONCOMBATANT SERVICE
or unzip a medium girl's forehead into the mud.

(15)
Life took to dirt as it took to water.

Once, the planet was all stone & fire.

Then dirt.   Then perpetual ocean,
which is not a question of power.

Then an animal staggered onto dirt
with uncertain limbs,
became Eve.

Then you.
Then dirt eye.

(UNLESS EXEMPTED THEREFROM).

(16)

The birds were VERIFYING WITNESSES of Lazarus.
The birds were Lazarus of the meteor.

They took flight
& escaped annihilation,
but not its SUPPLEMENTAL AFFIDAVIT.

They watched the wind bruise the chestnut trees,
& the chestnut trees drop their payloads.

The birds flew microfilm across enemy lines.

Then they were turned into hats.

Say:

once there was no country,
no treaties,
only mountains not yet weathered
by time's unrelenting melt.
No south.
No pen.
No metaphor.

There's comfort in myth.

Dirt eye is not a metaphor.

(17)

WHERETOFORE

I am dirt eye.

I SWEAR (AFFIRM)

I am dirt eye,

SO HELP ME GOD.

OATH OF ALLEGIANCE

I HEREBY DECLARE, ON OATH,
      THAT no state can ABSOLUTELY AND ENTIRELY
      archive the ocean which delivered us;

THAT I WILL BEAR
         the archive, the railroad spike,
         the tokens of jade & brilliance of the rising sun,

                  which make manna,
                  which makes a name;

THAT I WILL PERFORM
           resurrection in the name of insurrecting joy;

THAT I WILL PERFORM
         the WORK OF the medium
           to floss our phantoms from the archive,

                  which is alchemy,
                  which is an ear;

& THAT I TAKE THIS OBLIGATION FREELY
      & in the indicative mood: our future,

                  which is *both/and,*
                  which is soil,
                  which is here.

We are here,

SO HELP ME GOD.

Petition granted and Certificate No. ....10943781.................... issued.
Petition denied: List No. ....

☆ U.S. GOVERNMENT PRINTING OFFICE: 1960–672-804

CAROLYN FLYNN

A RECIPE FOR DESIRE

Our father had been gone three months, and this whole time I've been wanting my mother to teach me how to make a hummingbird cake. I think he's still in America, but if he isn't, where he is could be the Caribbean islands, which is where I guess they first made hummingbird cake. I only think that because the cake is made from pineapple and banana. It's sweet, like the nectar hummingbirds feast upon. Imagine, living your whole life on nectar, and nectar only. That's what hummingbirds do.

The cake my mother makes wears a confident streak of golden banana like a pollinator sweeping through a garden. It's got the taste of another place. A place that isn't New Orleans, a place that hasn't been left behind. My mother needed that, and I would learn how to make this cake so I could give it to her anytime she needed it.

Even though my mother made hummingbird cake for Réveillon and sometimes in late winter just when we doubted spring would ever come, it was always Grandma Grace's recipe in our minds. Grace's hummingbird cake was artfully prepared as her watercolors, teeming with dots of plum and apricot and lemon colors that bled into each other and made me wish I knew her before she knew my grandfather. She'd had loved him for 50 years—two lifetimes, she says. I wanted to know who she was before she loved, because that's who I was now. I wanted to know her pure desire, test if the stories she passed to me were genuine. With hummingbird cake, the boundary between moist cake and creamy frosting was just an idea someone had once had, a separate-but-not-equal co-existence. Because frosting always tasted better. This cake was an exuberant mouthful of bayou magic, land seduced into sea. This cake, somehow, contained our history.

I was twelve, and only just beginning to notice that sometimes I desired people and they didn't desire me. What I didn't know was that my mother had made a vow she could not live this way. I only knew that if I made her this cake, we could keep things in place.

Start with your shopping list, she told me the day she agreed but I think she was just stalling. You need to know what you want and exactly how much you want. You need to know which vendors will be stocking and selling what you want. You want the best, freshest ingredients. Fresh is what makes the difference in every dish you make. If you use dried or frozen ingredients, all the bright flavor will be lost. That's your mission with a hummingbird cake, above all, to hold the brightness. I presented her a list.

Second, know where to find the best ingredients, she conceded with a settling of her shoulders. Make friends with your vendors. Ask about their supplies. Ask: What makes the thyme smokier, the oysters more tender, the French bread crisper? When do the best oysters come in? You don't want the other oysters. Sprinkle your desire with discernment. Know what you want, know what you don't want.

So you save yourself, she said, from culinary disaster. You don't have to make oyster stew that day when the bad oysters come in or the day they don't come in at all. Or if you insist it will be an oyster day, make oyster po'boys.

At last, I'd gotten her to the kitchen. There we were, aprons on, and she was saying, this cake depends on mashed bananas and crushed pineapple. Retain all the juices. Use vegetable oil, not butter. These were confident, clear instructions. This woman who doubted herself so many times, she was proving me wrong about all the reasons I wanted to grow up faster and leave her.

Third, what fails in the kitchen stays in the kitchen. Only share your taste-worthy work. Don't over-mix. Just combine, she said, slowing my hand. Otherwise you knock out all the air and replace it with gluten. That makes the cake too dense.

We started over.

Fourth, and with this she tossed a pear-gold curl from her brow, in the sexy way I'd seen women do in the movies when they know they have a man's eyes on their face, remember always that cooking is chemistry. Air is part of the chemistry. Your creations must breathe. It's not about assembly. It's about how the flavors blend.

Fifth, cooking is about attention. A lot of people like to talk about their secret ingredient. Everyone has one. For some, it's cloves but the cloves must be from Madagascar. For others, it's white-tea infused macadamia milk or champagne sugar.

But that's not the secret. It's about attentiveness. The secret ingredient is devotion. The secret is to let yourself desire what you desire and allow yourself to give your attention to it. You need to be there at the stovetop stirring the caramelizing white chocolate so that just the moment before it blooms with that caramel color, you are prepared to take it off the heat. So many times, it's about too much heat. Inattentiveness.

Then and only then do you add your distinctive touch.

Grace always adds a hint of citrus to the frosting, my mother told me. That gave the cake a brightness. Grace was always bright. How was that possible?

With all that moist sweetness, I wanted to add something to hold it. I would add a sweet crunch, with a praline brittle topping. I smashed the pralines into crumbs and sprinkled them across the soft peaks of cream cheese frosting.

As my mother tasted it, she said, this is phenomenal. I never knew hummingbird cake could taste like this.

When is our father coming back? I wanted to know as my thumb raked the bits of brittle from my plate and dusted my slice of cake with a renewed rain of topping.

Marriages are a lot of work, our mother says. But I don't want to know about her marriage because her marriage is to our father, and I'm still trying to love him.

KYLE IMPINI

A SONG FOR MRS. HARRIS

I was friends with Bradley Harris for more reasons than that his mom let us play M-rated video games, but it was a factor. My mother never would have allowed *Halo* in our house, emblazoned as it was with its crude warning: Mature, 17+. Mrs. Harris, though, didn't seem to mind the violence. She even seemed interested in the game. Her questions felt like genuine curiosity, not the sly investigations I would've suffered at home. Sometimes, after finishing a cigarette out on the porch, she lingered in the living room, watching us play.

"Who's that?" she would ask, gesturing to the screen where Bradley and I detonated grenades and chased down retreating grunts. Bradley would respond with a terseness I was surprised she allowed. She'd go on with her questioning, asking for the names of vehicles and characters, sometimes pondering the root cause of all this violence. "What's it for?" she'd ask. "Why all this fighting?" The more open-ended her questions grew, the sharper Bradley's responses became. The interactions usually terminated with Bradley growling at his mom in an irritated, remonstrative tone that made me go tense in expectation of a slap or a scold. Instead, Mrs. Harris dismissed her son with a click of her tongue and a flick of her hand, like she was shooing away a fly.

For twelve consecutive Sundays, Bradley and I played *Halo*. He, miraculously, did not play the game's campaign without me, an act of selflessness I still marvel at. This, I think, was evidence of his true nature, a nature our teachers seldom saw. Though nothing but kind to me, he was gruff and knew curse words and was quick to anger. Moreover, he was unlucky in his looks; he just looked like a bully. Stocky with a square face and dull, deep-set eyes, he was big for his age, and the other students liked to say he had been held back a year or two. He was prideful and got in a lot of fights. Though few were his fault, he always received the harsher punishment. If a harried, underpaid teacher had a split-second to assign blame to one of two brawling third-graders, they would pick him.

One week, he got in a particularly rough scrap and earned himself two days of in-school suspension. My first thought after hearing the news was of *Halo*; we were stuck between the second and third reactor cores on "Two Betrayals," and I was sure he'd be grounded. At church on Sunday, I prayed for forgiveness for Bradley, forbearance from his parents, and the continued ignorance of my own. When I arrived home, I called their house and considered my prayers answered when Mrs. Harris told me to come on over, that Bradley was waiting for me.

After we'd made a few attempts at stealing the Banshees, Bradley's dad came into the room. Mr. Harris usually worked on Sundays and kept to himself when he didn't. He played drums in a band and smelled like beer and gasoline. His tattoos and goatee made me embarrassed of my own father. He started talking, but Bradley didn't spit out a remonstrative *dad*. He paused the game and we listened dutifully. Mr. Harris asked me if I knew what had happened at school with Bradley.

I did. Another student had made fun of the thin gold necklace Bradley wore every day. The necklace was a gift from his father, who had told him it was real gold. Bradley must have known in his heart of hearts that the thing was fake, but I never heard him admit it. Our classmate had informed him that the necklace wasn't real and that people won plastic junk like that at the state fair all the time. Bradley asked the kid if he was calling his dad a liar. The kid shrugged and Bradley lunged.

I nodded to Mr. Harris.

He smiled and asked if I had seen the fight for myself.

I nodded again. I had seen the tail end of it. Bradley had just gotten on top of the other kid, pinning his arms to the ground. Though it meant serious consequences for Bradley, I was glad when I saw the teacher supervising recess running toward them. If the teacher hadn't intervened, Bradley would've taken it too far.

"How'd my boy do?"

Mr. Harris grinned at me. I wasn't sure if it was a trick question. I turned to Bradley, who stared up at his father, face bright, full of expectation.

"Pretty good," I said.

"That's what I like to hear."

Mr. Harris smiled and looked to his son, greedy pride streaking across his face. He edged toward us, hands brought up to his chest at attention.

"We've got a little Jet Li over here."

He neared Bradley and started throwing out open-handed jabs at his stomach. Bradley dropped his controller and tried to block the jabs, which came faster and harder. Bradley giggled and pulled his legs up to protect himself, and Mr. Harris scooped him from the couch to the floor. The glasses on the coffee table trembled as Mr. Harris pinned Bradley the same way Bradley had the boy. I thought little of it. It was roughhousing, more similar than different to the kind of foolishness my father and I engaged in. Bradley's giggles slowed, then stopped as he tried to squirm his way free from his father, but soon he was trapped. He tapped the ground three times, and Mr. Harris rolled off him and stood, a little out of breath. Bradley panted on the ground.

"You know, in the real world," Mr. Harris said, "it's always the winner who gets tossed from the bar."

Mr. Harris brought his finger to his temple and tapped it, suggesting we commit this fact to memory.

Bradley and I watched rain fall on his new trampoline. We pressed our noses to the glass of his sliding back door, like two dogs who wanted out. During the school week, I had spent my recesses listening to Bradley brag about the feats he could accomplish on it—the backflips and jackknifes and three-sixties. I knew he was bullshitting about his abilities, but his talk titillated the hell out of me. I wanted on the thing. On my bike ride to his house, the rain started, fast and hard, and I could have cried with frustration.

We didn't even bother to boot up *Halo*. We just watched the rain and let our breath fog up the door.

"Would you look at that."

Mrs. Harris stalked up from behind us. She watched for a moment and let out a sigh. She was apparently the type to whom rain did something, something vague that hurt a pleasing little pain. She pressed her palm to the door.

"It's warm outside."

She slipped her arm between us and opened the door. The air came in, thick and steaming and a little intoxicating.

"My God," Mrs. Harris said with something like a shudder. She stuck her bare forearm over us and into the rain. Another sigh. She brought her arm back in and soon a cigarette was lighted behind us.

"You two want out or what?"

We looked up at her. She grinned slightly. The smoke unfurling from her lips looked like steam. She raised her eyebrows in the direction of the trampoline.

"Just take your socks off."

Out into the rain we tumbled. It was a forgiving rain, one of those late-spring downpours whose droplets feel just a degree or two warmer than your skin. We slipped through the mud and soon the barks of Bradley's two dogs sounded from the door. We fell, giggling and rolling as they caught up and leapt on us. They snapped at us with play-biting jaws and twisted their legs up with our own. Mrs. Harris laughed in a careening, reckless way before whistling the dogs off us. Bradley and I slid beneath the protective netting of the trampoline and onto its surface. I doubt either of us landed more than a few consecutive jumps. We resorted to pushing each other into the netting. Mrs. Harris stood out in the lawn, the dogs circling her, licking at her hands like she had treats, while she laughed at our flailing. The rain turned her hair the darkest shade of blonde I'd ever seen it. Only after lightning struck and thunder clapped within five seconds of each other did she call us in. We stayed at the threshold while she fetched us towels. She swaddled us in them and allowed us into the now frigid air conditioning of the house.

The Harris's household confirmed my suspicion that the rules of my parents proceeded from hollow tradition—an empty sense of obligation to some rigid ideal. I can still remember how Mrs. Harris would put a hand over the phone and call out, "Your father's about to leave work; anything you two want from McDonald's?" nearly every Sunday. The melody of her question has been imprinted on my mind. I remember brownies—brownies as consolation, brownies as celebration; any occasion worth marking she marked with a tray. She was not much of a cook—most of the food I consumed in the house went from freezer to oven to plate—but I liked her food more than what my parents made. The dogs, too, were evidence of their freedom. Mrs. Harris purchased the first—an Australian Shepherd—to appease a six year old Bradley, and the second—a poodle—to satisfy some vague inner desire of hers. My parents would have only conceivably gotten me a dog as a living lesson in responsibility.

The rain didn't let up, so I shoved my bike into the back seat of Mrs. Harris's car, and she drove me home, just in time for a dinner for which my appetite had been spoiled. My mother met me at the door, and I walked in while Mrs. Harris explained why I held a bag of damp clothes and was wearing an AC/DC t-shirt. My mother stood and listened and was quick to say goodbye. She inspected me. She plucked up the shoulder of my shirt with a thumb and forefinger, sniffed it, and told me that I smelled like a bowling alley.

I had never heard shouting in a house before. Before that day in Bradley's room, I had only ever heard the human voice reach its full strength outdoors. Without room to expand and dissipate, the screams stayed in, trapped by the house, and stewed into a malevolence that infected its very walls. It made me think of ants and rats and termites and cockroaches and all the persistent, insidious vermin that turn houses wretched. It made me think of the way mold proliferates, how in its patient, mindless way it infects and consumes. The screams clawed their way out from the master bedroom and dominated the house. The air felt changed, thick and heady and unsafe to breathe. I was caught between the desire to listen close and plug my ears. I set down my controller and looked to Bradley. His eyes stayed fixed on the screen. Soon, he noticed that I'd stopped playing, that he was fighting alone.

"Dude," he said. "I can't beat this without you."

I picked up my controller, and we played through, even after the shouts climaxed with a smack, even after the yelling turned to a lone whimper, even after the front door slammed.

I avoided Bradley. I could sense the sickness of his house on him. At recess, he would hound me down and try to convince me that what had happened was no big deal. He spoke about the incident and resulting divorce casually. His nonchalance, though likely an affectation, disturbed me. His invitations became increasingly desperate until one day he got the message. Without me to distract him, he got in more scraps and arguments. I made other friends, but it wasn't the same. Our interactions seemed stiff. Still, their houses were clean and quiet, and my parents chatted amiably with theirs.

A year passed this way, until, one night, I watched the local news with my mother. It was after dinner, and she was sipping her nightly glass of wine. The anchor spoke of a liquor store robbery gone wrong. It had ended with a homicide. They showed the mugshots of the three suspects. All were still in high school; the getaway driver hadn't even graduated from learner's permit to driver's license. A reporter interviewed the mother of the one who had pulled the trigger. She wept in her child's bedroom. The cameraman, either collecting simple B-roll or making a point, panned over the killer's game collection. He lingered at the end, on the spine of *Grand Theft Auto: San Andreas.*

"Oh, that game," my mother said. "Dreadful. Have you heard of it?"

Of course I had. It was 2005. The game was the great forbidden. I nodded and my mom shook her head and looked back to the screen.

"Just awful," she said.

At recess the next day, I approached Bradley. I asked him if he owned *San Andreas.* He smiled.

By our sophomore year of high school, my mother had capitulated: violent video games were grudgingly allowed. Still, I didn't stop going over to Bradley's. The forbidden pleasures of the mature hardly ended with *Grand Theft Auto*.

We were fifteen and had apparently smoked everything besides genuine marijuana—oregano, tea leaves, spice, his mom's Camels—and we finally had what seemed to be the real deal. It was a Saturday, and his mom was holed up in the library of Ivy Tech Community College, studying for her nursing exams. His father was gone; he sent checks on Christmas and Bradley's birthday. We emptied half the tobacco from a Camel, and, fingers shaky with anticipation, refilled it with weed. We worked with the focus and precision of bomb defusers. The process could not have taken more than a couple minutes, but I remember it as a protracted enterprise with multiple stages and setbacks. Finally, we had it full. We tamped its tip down with the sharpened end of a pencil, opened a window, and smoked.

Five minutes passed, then ten, then fifteen, and I felt no discernable difference in body or mind. Perhaps the music issuing from Bradley's speakers felt more present, but it was nothing I couldn't have chalked up to placebo. We shrugged—by now so used to disappointment—and booted up *Halo 3*'s matchmaking. It was not until I heard the game's theme music—those sonorous, monkish drones—that I knew something was different. It felt ancient and holy. The game now seemed incidental to the music. Why move past the menu screen? I looked to Bradley, and we met eyes, grinning like lunatics, less pleased with the feeling itself than that we had finally made it, that another veil between us and what we perceived to be adulthood had been torn as we inched our way to the holy of holies, a truth so simple and terrifying it must be experienced instead of learned.

The front door open and closed, and that now-familiar miasma descended on me. Heavy footfalls proceeded up the stairs. For the first of many times, I discovered the difficulty—the insanity—of trying to act natural.

Mrs. Harris swung open the door.

"Out," she said. "Both of you."

She stood in the doorway while we marched past her. She turned and followed us down the stairs to the living room.

"Sit," she said, motioning to the couch.

Bradley started to protest, and Mrs. Harris just stared at him. We sat. She went to the kitchen and returned with a straight-backed chair. She sat down before us and buried her face in her hands. With her face down, I saw the brownish roots of her hair. Their darkness startled me. All these years she had not been a natural blonde. She looked up, hands still covering her mouth and nose, and I saw her eyes. She looked older than I had remembered; I had always thought of her as young. She had usually been the youngest mom at any school event. Her youth had been a subject of suspicion and gossip for the other parents, an explanation for her son's behavior. The math wasn't difficult; she had been nineteen when she gave birth to Bradley. It was unfortunate that our adolescence coincided with the popularity of MTV's Teen Mom. Mrs. Harris bore a passing resemblance to one of the show's stars, and our classmates learned that to get a rise out of Bradley and have him embarrass himself, they need only ask how "Mackenzie" was doing. The jokes proliferated. The chorus to "Stacy's Mom" was crudely and effectively changed to "Bradley's Mom." In late middle school, when our classmates had started watching *American Pie* at low volume, listening for the footsteps of their parents, we observed a case of independent discovery; all thought to apply the word they learned—MILF—to Mrs. Harris.

I had been unable to see past this designation. Before then, I hadn't understood her as I did other moms. She possessed beauty, and, I figured, all its attendant pleasures. But now I saw that life had aged her, that she was not protected from its ravages. She looked terribly, terribly tired. She exhaled a sigh so deep I was surprised she didn't deflate. Since Mr. Harris had left, she had been working days at a call center and spending nights in classes. Now, she was in the final year of her nursing degree, her exams looming, a mere month away.

"I know what you two were doing."

We sat there, silent. She seemed like she was going to admonish us, but she just started crying.

❖

Mrs. Harris's tears did not stop our experiments. Once the shock of seeing a grown woman cry at length faded, all that was left was the glee of getting away with it. We moved our experiments outside.

She must've known what we were up to when we told her we were "going on a walk," a baggie and some of her pilfered cigarettes in our pockets, but she didn't let on that she did. She kept her nose in her books. As much as the arrangement confused me, I didn't question it. I was happy for the freedom and unaware that adults operated under the same delusions I did, that Mrs. Harris truly believed that after finals, everything would click into place. She'd find it easy to quit smoking. She'd replace soda with water. She'd sit Bradley down and tell an illuminating and disturbing tale of her own involvement with drugs and nip his use in the bud. Maybe she'd even start dating in the dignified, forthright manner of middle-aged professionals. It was a necessary delusion, that completing one task could solve so many others. Its elegance staved off hopelessness.

Her books drew her into a private world and sapped her energy and attention and patience. She snapped over small things—soda cans left on the coffee table, housekeys misplaced—and let the big things slide. She was so close. It was almost over. Soon she would no longer have to sit in a room of chittering twenty-somethings, with their unwrinkled skin and their fiancés and their first houses and first dogs and first break-ups—their whole lives a procession of firsts, a parade of novelty, while she, dear Mrs. Harris, bore the last name of a man she communicated with through a lawyer.

As her exam date neared, an ambient, low-level hum of tension surrounded her and corrupted the things she said and the food she made. When Bradley asked if I could spend the night the evening before her exams, she bristled but didn't say no. Bradley and I, as usual, stayed up deep into the night, playing game after game of *Halo* matchmaking. Around two in the morning, I tiptoed downstairs to nab some chips from the pantry. I heard retching in the bathroom. More out of curiosity than concern, I rapped on the door with a knuckle and asked if she was okay. The toilet flushed and soon the faucet ran. Mrs. Harris emerged. Her face was wet. She said "Hello," in a distant, formal way. I didn't know what to say. She clutched at the collar of her shirt and looked at the floor.

"I keep on having this dream that I overslept for my exam. It's waking me up every thirty minutes. Every time I start to drift off, the dream snaps me out of it. I feel nuts."

Her eyes skittered around like insects trapped in jars. I told her I was sorry. She breathed in, and then lunged at me. She hugged me, but it took me a moment to put my arms around her. It felt like she was extracting something she needed from me. She held me like that, like some desperate dancer, and let go. She wiped her nose and went to her room without another word.

The day after Mrs. Harris received her exam results, she asked Bradley and me to move the TV from the living room to her bedroom.

"Nobody uses it out here," she said. "You two always play on the one in your room, and I don't want to watch my shows in the middle of you two running around. The TV being here only makes sense if we had company over, and we never have company. I'm tired of pretending we ever have company."

She sat on the edge of her bed while we lugged the thing into her room. We set it up on her dresser, right in front of her bed, and that was the last I saw of her for three weeks.

The closest I came to her was when Bradley would crack the door and inform her in his meekest, gentlest voice that we were going on a walk or to McDonald's or to the park. The TV rattled on. Occasionally she responded. The stillness of the air that issued from the room gave me an idea of its state, and future experiences with despair—the despair of family members, roommates, girlfriends, and my own—would complete the picture. I can imagine the way glasses would've accumulated on her nightstand and how dirty tissues would mark the side of the bed she favored. I can imagine ashtrays like porcupines, the take-out bags littering the floor, and how dirty clothing would spread out from an overflowing hamper like sartorial mold. As her despair went on, the sickness metastasized to the kitchen. Soon the sink overflowed with precarious stacks of dishes, their grease and scraps and residues mingling and multiplying. Lightbulbs went unchanged and cast a twilit dimness over the house. The dogs were unwalked and jumpy; the windows turned opaque from their breath.

Bradley and I lived in the space that Mrs. Harris's withdrawal created; our world expanded as hers contracted. I understood on some deep level that something was wrong, but I was fifteen and it was summer; it didn't seem fair that this should interfere with my life. We lived around the mess. Our weed-smoking turned casual, habitual. We no longer stole off to do it. We no longer packed his small, blackened bowl with care and reverence. We got high and went on with it.

We grew bolder. We had girls over. When one of them—Sarah—asked if anyone was home, Bradley told the truth: that his mom was in her room but would not emerge even if we smoked. The two girls looked to each other, each asking the other what they had gotten themselves into. It took them a few visits, but soon they became comfortable. They supplied beer and we supplied weed.

It was on the Harris's couch with Mrs. Harris, that shade, trapped in her room that I first explored a woman's body. We had all been drinking beer in Bradley's room and watching late-night infomercials for the smutty DVDs he had gotten in trouble for ordering a year or so before. Bradley and Sarah started, so Cindy and I went downstairs. Why Sarah picked Bradley or Cindy picked me is a mystery. In three years, she'd go to DePauw on scholarship. In seven more, she'd graduate with a law degree. I showed no such potential, but I didn't think it was odd she was after me. I now think that the girls must've discussed it all in advance. I imagine a pact solemnly sealed, straws drawn. Bradley and I were interchangeable, means to an end. But I didn't think that then. I thought I deserved everything that came to me. We stained the couch. Cindy and I cleaned it up, giggling, but the outlines remained.

A week passed, and already Cindy and Sarah were bored with us. They left directly after smoking, with flimsy excuses. Bradley took it in stride. Due to either insensitivity or wisdom, he knew better than to fight the inevitable. I didn't. I fought gravity and planned a last-ditch effort. Cindy's birthday was approaching, and I asked her if she wanted to come over to Bradley's to celebrate. She told me she had plans with family, but that she'd let me know. I was too inexperienced to know what this meant.

I waited at the Harris's on Cindy's birthday, a big bundle of nerves, playing *Halo* with Bradley. I checked my phone every time I died.

"You've got to stop," Bradley said.

"Fuck off."

"She's not coming over."

I ran from this truth. I doubled down. I had to do something special. I left Bradley to his game and rifled around the kitchen, looking for something fun. I wrinkled my nose against the viney growths springing from potatoes and the blackened bananas, sickly, shriveled, still hanging on the banana stand from gnarled stems. I looked through the cabinets, clearing away bags of rice and boxes of pasta, and spotted a box of brownie mix. It was festive. I remembered when this was what indulgence meant. The warmth of being swaddled in a fresh towel after emerging from warm spring rain washed over me. I inspected the box's label and was pleased to find it required little besides the mix itself. I closed the cabinet and got to it.

My work soon multiplied. The few dishes I needed were already dirty, and in order to clear enough space in the sink to clean them, I would have to wash a cabinet's worth of dishes. I experienced a rush of gritty nostalgia upon seeing the scraps of meals I had consumed weeks ago. Soon the dishwasher was full and the mixture in the oven. I went back up to Bradley's room and saw my phone blinking. Bradley paused his game and watched my face fall. Cindy would not be able to make it over. I understood the message's implications. I flopped onto his bed.

"Fuck everything."

"I told you, man."

He said it tenderly, like he had been trying to protect me from this disappointment. I didn't even bother with telling him off. I lay there in the bed, and the disparity between Cindy and me presented itself as a cold arrangement of facts. The oven timer went off, and its ring reminded me how foolish I had been those fifteen minutes ago, how plucky, how naïve, how stupid. I trudged down the steps and pulled the brownies from the oven. Their dull, brown surface looked as desolate as the moon. I wanted to do something stupid—to clatter the tray to the floor or grab two great fistfuls of the cooling stuff and throw it at the wall. I held my hands over the tray, but approaching footsteps brought them back to my sides. I turned, expecting a stoned and hungry Bradley, but instead there stood Mrs. Harris.

She wore a long bathrobe the shade of white a garment gets after too many washings. It was pilly and hung to her heels. Under the robe she wore a wife beater and what looked like men's boxers. She closed her robe and crossed her arms.

"Sorry," she said. She looked around. "I thought I smelled brownies."

She looked to the sink and saw it empty. On the table, too, she saw empty space, tidiness. She made connections and drew implications. She breathed in and looked to me, a hand over her heart. I encouraged her misconception. It made me feel like I had a handle on something.

"Want some?" I asked, slicing the mass into portions.

She sat down, and I put a square on a plate and set it before her. She laughed a little at the brownie. Her eyes still drooped with private dramas. I worried I had made a mistake. Maybe Mrs. Harris had sunk to that place where even taking a stab at happiness feels itself sad or embarrassing or pointless. I worried she saw a sick irony in all things sweet. She raised her fork like it was heavy and cut a piece and took a bite. Something kindled in her eyes. She emitted a sound—almost a laugh, but too small to be a laugh; it was the nearest thing to a giggle someone as deep in the hole as she was could produce. She covered her mouth in a dainty, refined way.

"Oh," she said. "That's rich."

She made a contented little noise in her throat and looked at me over her hand, still covering her mouth, eyes bright as if we now shared some understanding, some secret.

JOHN SIBLEY WILLIAMS

HEIRLOOM

—after Georgia O'Keeffe's "Wave Night," 1928

tonight is a small canvas that never entirely burns, or dims : a dark sky
severed from a darker earth : the only light knives the deep belly
of this unnamed, not-yet-consecrated body : how is it my daughters
after all that drowning kicked their way free of us, someday maybe
entirely : why does convex or concave depend on the angle we love
from : pregnant or miscarried : moonlit or lamp- : heirloom or shame,
how so much depends on the giver : in this version, it's coyotes
my great-grandfather shoos from the yard with a flaming cross :
in this version, what he handed down deserves a place on our mantle :
from so far beneath, these depths might just be heaven : looking up
past history, past forgiveness, the horizon is a dull circle separating
nothing : beautiful & nonexistent, the stars mark a pilgrim's path
from one to another impossible home : that there is anything here
worth loving, I whittle into my children's dreams with the broad
blade of my arms, can be called a blessing : depending on if we survive
it, tonight can be a mirror, or window : a door can be a wall lining
the southern lip of a country, or an aperture : eventually—I hope
they believe me when I say it—everyone burns their own imperfect stars
                                        into this cold, blue, unempty sky

JOHN SIBLEY WILLIAMS

SKYSCRAPE

is what my daughter,
whose body once believed

itself a boy's, in all her
uncertainty & sweetness,

calls every plumed white
contrail, every rafter briefly

holding the sky in its place.
That her twin sister angles

her dark eyes up to that same
aftermath, once it's dissolved,

& says where did all our rivers
go hurts more than the real

river that once cut our town
in half & now snakes dry &

heavy with shattered jars &
blown tires & all those unkept

promises of water. Of reflections.
Our bridges now with nothing to do

but span & spider. Because the world
is always about to end, I ask them what

they see when the bedroom goes
dark & the echo of my lullabies

fades to eulogy & all that's left is
the plumed white breath of winter

entering, unrequested, reminding
them of sky. & scrape. & lost rivers.

& she says I don't even see
my body anymore. Only what

my body will be someday. Around her
my arms grow too heavy to steeple,

nearly too soft to bridge. As overhead
all signs disappear. & all wounds.

As if the world is readying itself for us.
For her. As the planes keep crossing over

our brows, briefly, lovingly, like ash.

HANNAH SWARD

NOBODY WANTS A CRYING STRIPPER

Cinnamon. Honey. Cat. Beth. Who am I? Irina or Ava? I can't remember. At first I serve drinks. Diet coke and apple juice. No liquor or beer. It's all nude. Only topless places serve alcohol. I wear blue and white checkered Swiss Alps outfit. White knee socks. Black patent leather heels. Two braids. Girls dance. Men watch. I take orders for juice.

I stop serving soda. Start giving lap dances in the back with Rilke, my little sister. And shower dances. We don't like being hosed down.

We have a routine at The Wild Goose. Go to 24-Hour Fitness at noon on Gower. Go home. Get ready for work. Hair in rollers. Shave legs. Dark eyes. Glossy pink lips.

After a summer we move onto The Gentleman's Club. Prettier girls. More money. More competition; Celeste with her little tanned bum. Big auburn hair. Fake boobs and black patent leather thigh boots. Beth. Blonde hair, boobs, long legs. Lily, the tiny Asian. Looks fourteen. Wears bobby socks, pleated school uniform mini skirts. Dusty with her nude splits, back flips and tricks on the pole. Taylor and her fishnet skin suit. Candy just walks out onstage nude with her bare feet and boobs.

Daytime girls. A little heavier. A little older. While daytime men eat stale lunchtime pizza strip special. These girls have kids. Make less money, dance at two pm on Wednesdays for regulars. Big Red himself comes in at four p.m. in his blue and white overalls. Sits on a stool.

Supply of Big Red chewing gum on the bar table. Stays until closing. Having a slow day? You can count on Big Red paying for a dance, can always count on him for a dance.

I avoid cute, younger guys who come in on a Saturday night for bachelor parties. Not sure I'm pretty enough to ask if they want a dance. Businessmen, city workers. Asian men who come on buses. They all like me, and I'm sure to make money when I see the buses. White men don't like me. They like Beth, Taylor, and Dusty who look like this is really fun to do.

In the Gentlemen's Club my name is Claudia. Rilke is Lola. We seem to do well in the beginning. They like to see us together.

"If Claudia and Lola don't do well," the girls used to say," You know it's a bad night."

Maybe it's slow for us now because we don't buy clothes at Fredrick's of Hollywood like the other girls. We wear bras and undies from Marshalls. Eat rice cakes, frozen yogurt, and sticky rice. After, we go to IHOP on Santa Monica Boulevard for blueberry pancakes. And we are curvier than the other girls. We never see them eat. Maybe we should lose weight.

We do meth for a month. Don't eat. We're in a bad mood. Get clumsy onstage, losing balance. And don't lose a pound. Everybody loses weight on meth. Not us. We get on phen phen. A diet drug. Get skinnier like Dusty, Celeste, and Beth.

We think we look better. Cut our long hair.

Make even less money. Buy hundred-dollar wigs on Hollywood Boulevard. Me, a platinum blonde long wig with bangs that shifts to one side when I dance. Rilke, a chestnut fall, attached to the back of her head; she swings it around like a sexy pony onstage.

I start to sit on the side. Cry. Lola, she seems to do alright with her good dancing and ponytail wig. Not me. I get real sensitive and sad. Taking my phen phen. Getting skinnier and skinnier. Sitting there with my big blonde Hollywood Boulevard wig.

I have Frank, though. He followed me from The Wild Goose to The Gentleman's Club. He never asks the other girls for a dance. He only comes to see me. First as Irina or Ava or whatever my name was at The Wild Goose. Now as Claudia. I wanted to be Alexis but that name was already taken. Frank brings me flowers, Shalimar, and money for private dances. An Asian architect with a big belly, he wants to bring me to The Magic Castle for dinner and shopping at Victoria's Secret. But I keep it to the club and private dances. Sometimes I let him touch me when the bouncer isn't looking.

There is another man who comes to see me regular. I think he is a director at the studio nearby. He is quiet and doesn't sit at the stage. Tall and thin with gray hair in a short ponytail, narrow nose and small eyes that look like they see a lot. I liked him right away. He comes in, sits at the bar and orders an apple juice. I never go up to him. Let him take his time.

Today after his juice he starts walking to the back. I follow him behind the black velvet curtain, take his long thin hand, and lead him to a mirrored private dance booth with the fake red leather chair.

Doc, the bouncer, an ex-football player has his hand on the black velvet curtain. He sees me straddle the director in my Swedish barmaid outfit until the song is over. I had sex with Doc once. I didn't know he had a fiancée. She climbed through the window and chased me out. I ran through the yard with his litter of pit bulls running after me and barking.

After work Rilke and I go to a Japanese restaurant between the studio and the club. We pull on our green hospital pants that we always wear, t-shirts, and knot our hair on top of our heads so it sprays out like fountains. There is the director eating sushi with a woman and a little girl. I go right up to him with my sticky rice in a white paper bag and say,

"Hi."

He just stares at me. I never see him again.

❖

Rilke and I don't spend so much time together since she met Jeremiah. AKA Squid. We met Squid at a daytime drug party in Sun Valley. A 1970's house with fake grass, sliding glass doors, and a cement back yard. The party looked boring. Ten people lying on the couch, standing around, leaning against the fridge. A girl with blonde hair, red pleated mini skirt, and bare feet blended us a mushroom shake. We'd done everything, but not mushrooms. Rilke drank hers out of a coffee cup. I drank mine out of a white mug. It said, 'number one granny'. We waited for the hit from the mushrooms. Went to the bathroom. As we took turns peeing we both fell on the furry bright green bath mat laughing. Back to the kitchen. That's when Squid walked in and looked at us. His hair buzzed close to his scalp. What hair there is, is dyed leopard.

"Want to see something?" he asked.

He zips down his zipper. Pulls out his uncircumcised dick. Takes a pencil from his back pocket. Sticks it through his pierced foreskin. Rilke and Squid liked each other right off.

Squid visits her at the Gentleman's Club. Spends the night at our place. I hear them having sex in the living room. And again more sex. He locks himself in the bathroom coughing and running the water. Squid is a heroin addict. Calls Rilke from jail one day to get him. I go with her. His mother shows up. Takes us all for chocolate chip pancakes at IHOP on Santa Monica Boulevard. In the middle Squid gets sick. He leaves. We sit there with Squid's mother. Pour more fake maple syrup on our pancakes. We don't know what to say.

Squid lives in Sylmar, far as you can go in the valley, with his grandma who writes bad checks. He has the bedroom. She wears muumuu dresses with bunny prints, makes chocolate boxed cake, and sleeps on the couch. On the other couch is another grandma. They call each other grandma. At night they push the couches side by side. Daytime, they sit in that house in Sylmar.

While Rilke and Squid have sex and fight, more sex, drive back from Los Feliz to Sylmar, then Sylmar to Los Feliz and back for more sex, I lose weight and lose my shape. Phen phen from doctors in Korea Town. The Valley. Western Boulevard. Wear electric blue jogging pants. Gray flannels underneath. I fry up three or four bags a day of frozen vegetables with curry from the Armenian market. Kitchen is painted black. The only sound, cars on Franklin Boulevard. I am depressed.

Rilke moves out with Squid. She said go anywhere but Miracle Mile. I find a one-bedroom in Miracle Mile. Landlady, Bertha, is Jewish and old.

"Honey, you strip for a living?" she asks. "You move in. I know you make money. But no visitors."

She means it. No visitors. She monitors the front entrance in her blue fuzzy slippers. Short thin red hair standing on end.

I have the back corner apartment with industrial carpeting. Looking out the two large living room windows, I can open the screen and touch the stucco. Same view from the kitchen. Kitchen is not black.

My bedroom overlooks the old neighbor in his yarmulke. He stands on his porch, thin pale legs in dingy boxers, he hangs wet undershirts on a wheel in a clothing line. On his windowsill old tapes play Klezmer mourning songs. He must've had a wife. I wonder when she died and how long this mourning music will go on. How much longer can I strip and eat curried vegetables?

I like this guy Eddie from New Mexico. I see him walking down the street, his dark hair hanging over his face, never looking up, only down at the pavement. He works at Buzz Coffee on Beverly Boulevard. I hope one day he likes me the way I like him. Sometimes he spends the night. He keeps his jeans on, and I keep my underwear on and we kiss. Once we played pool at Hollywood Billiards. I wore a blue cashmere dress. He said I looked pretty. Another time we went to the movies and it was raining.

"I think this could work," he said.

The next day he called me, "I can't see you anymore."

He hung up. I walked down the street with the cat someone left by my door. The cat had looked depressed. Knocked on his door and asked if the cat could stay at his place for the night. I wasn't really going anywhere. I just wanted to see him. I went back to my apartment. Sat in a butterfly chair, trying to block out the Klezmer music.

There's a knock at the door.

"Squid," Rilke cries, "I walked in on him shooting heroin."

She moves one street over from me. Cochran. Next to Staples and Sally's Beauty. Rilke and I share a 1988 Mazda. Every time we turn a corner it screeches. Sometimes we park it down the street so nobody sees us in it.

Rilke is trying to get over Squid. I am trying to quit stripping. I spend mornings calling into Central Office for extras to play in movies. Most of the time it's a recording.

"Call for homeless teens."

"Two African American males."

"Young, hip clubgoers and a Vietnam Vet type with no arm."

If I fit the description I go to the valley in the Mazda. If I don't fit I go to San Fernando Boulevard to strip.

CONTRIBUTORS

Gayle Brandeis (judge, Susan Atefat Prize for Creative Nonfiction) is the author, most recently, of the memoir *The Art of Misdiagnosis* (Beacon Press), and the novel-in-poems *Many Restless Concerns* (Black Lawrence Press). Earlier books include the poetry collection *The Selfless Bliss of the Body* (Finishing Line Press), the craft book *Fruitflesh: Seeds of Inspiration for Women Who Write* (HarperOne) and the novels *The Book of Dead Birds* (HarperCollins), which won the PEN/Bellwether Prize, *Self Storage* (Ballantine), *Delta Girls* (Ballantine), and *My Life with the Lincolns* (Henry Holt BYR). Her essay collection *Drawing/Breath* will be released by Overcup Press in 2023. She teaches in the MFA programs at Antioch University and Sierra Nevada University.

Marcus Cafagña is the author of three books of poetry, *The Broken World*, a National Poetry Series selection, *Roman Fever*, and *All the Rage in the Afterlife This Season*, forthcoming in 2023. His poems have also appeared in *Arts & Letters, Harvard Review, Quarterly West, Rattle, The Southern Review*, among others. Born in Michigan, he left Pennsylvania for the Ozarks.

Erin Carlyle is a poet living in Atlanta, Georgia. Her poetry often explores the connections between poverty, place, and girlhood, and can be found in journals such as *Tupelo Quarterly, Ruminate, Arts and Letters, Jet Fuel,* and *Prairie Schooner.* Her debut full-length collection, *Magnolia Canopy Otherworld*, 2020, is published on Driftwood Press. She is currently pursuing her PhD in Creative Writing at Georgia State University.

Donte Collins (they/them; b. Chicago Heights. 1996) is a neurodivergent afro-surrealist blues poet, playwright, and movement artist named the Inaugural Youth Poet Laureate of Saint Paul, Minnesota. They have received fellowships, scholarships, and awards from the Academy of American Poets, *the Adroit Journal,* the Mcknight Foundation, The National Urban League, The Dramatist Guild Foundation, *Frontier Poetry*, Augsburg University, *Indiana Review,* and *BOMB Magazine*. They are an alum of TruArtSpeaks, an arts & culture organization cultivating literacy, leadership, and social justice through the study & application of Spoken Word and Hip Hop culture. Their choreopoem, "Mercy," is forthcoming.

Carolyn Flynn is a memoirist, novelist, and essayist who was longlisted for the Mslexia International Memoir Prize for *Boundless*, a becoming-of-age memoir, and shortlisted for the Elixir Press First Novel Prize for *Searching for Persephone*. Her essays have been published in *Fourth Genre, Under the Gum Tree, The Colorado Sun, The Tampa Review, The Whitefish Review* (Montana Prize for Fiction), *Albuquerque Journal, Sage Magazine, Albuquerque the Magazine* and *Wilde Frauen*. A TEDx speaker ("Tell A Better Story, Live a Better Life"), she lives in Albuquerque, New Mexico, where she is a hiker and a pilgrim and an appreciator of horizons.

Vernita Hall is the author of *Where William Walked: Poems About Philadelphia and Its People of Color*, winner of the Willow Books Grand Prize and of the Robert Creeley Prize from Marsh Hawk Press; and *The Hitchhiking Robot Learns About Philadelphians*, winner of the Moonstone Press Chapbook Contest. Her poems have appeared or are forthcoming in *Poetry, American Poetry Review, African American Review, Barrow Street, The Common, River Styx, The Hopkins Review*, and *Obsidian*. She holds an MFA in Creative Writing from Rosemont College and serves on the poetry review board of *Philadelphia Stories*.

Kathryn Hargett-Hsu 徐凯蒂 is an MFA candidate in poetry at Washington University in St. Louis. Born and raised in Alabama, she is the recipient of fellowships from Kundiman, Fine Arts Work Center in Provincetown, the Bucknell Seminar for Undergraduate Poets, and the Mendocino Coast Writers Conference. Most recently, she received the Academy of American Poets Prize and the Lynda Hull Memorial Prize. Find her in *Best New Poets,*

Crazyhorse, Pleiades, Muzzle Magazine, The Margins, Salt Hill Journal, Cherry Tree, TaiwaneseAmerican.org, *The Adroit Journal,* and elsewhere.

W.J. Herbert's (Rumi Prize for Poetry) debut collection, *Dear Specimen,* (Beacon Press, 2021) was selected by Kwame Dawes as a winner of the 2020 National Poetry Series and was awarded a 2022 Maine Literary Award for Poetry. Chosen by Natasha Trethewey for inclusion in Best American Poetry 2017, Herbert's work also appears in *Alaska Quarterly Review, The Atlantic, The Hudson Review, Boulevard, Pleiades,* and elsewhere. Born in Cleveland, Ohio, she was raised in Southern California where she earned a bachelor's in studio art and a master's in flute performance. Herbert served for seven years as curator of the bimonthly poetry series and annual poetry competition offered by DA Center for the Arts in Pomona, California. She lives in Portland, Maine and Kingston, New York.

Kyle Impini graduated from Indiana University with degrees in English and History. His work has appeared in the *Bellevue Literary Review, Midwest Gothic, Sierra Nevada Review,* and elsewhere. He lives in Bloomington, Indiana with his fiancé and cat.

Allison Joseph (judge, Rumi Prize for Poetry) currently lives, teaches, and writes in Carbondale, Illinois, where she is a part of the creative writing faculty at Southern Illinois University. Her most recent collections of poems are *Lexicon* (Red Hen Press, 2021), *Professional Happiness* (Backbone Press, 2021), and *Confessions of a Bare Faced Woman* (Red Hen Press, 2018), which won the 2019 Feathered Quill Book Award and was a finalist in the poetry category for the NAACP Image Award. Her poems have appeared in *The New York Times* and the *Best American Poetry* series. She is the widow of poet and editor John Tribble.

Zoe Pappenheimer (Arts & Letters Prize for Fiction) is a graphic designer, illustrator and short-story writer originally from Seattle, WA. She lives in western Massachusetts with her husband and two kids.

Andrew Porter (judge, Arts & Letters Prize for Fiction) is the author of three books, including the forthcoming short story collection *The Disappeared* (Alfred A. Knopf, 2022), the short story collection *The Theory of Light and Matter* (Vintage/Penguin Random House), which won the Flannery O'Connor Award for Short Fiction, and the novel *In Between Days* (Knopf), which was a Barnes & Noble "Discover Great New Writers" selection and an IndieBound "Indie Next" selection. Porter's books have been published in foreign editions in the U.K. and Australia, and have been translated into numerous languages. Individual stories have appeared in such publications as *The Pushcart Prize anthology*, *Ploughshares*, *One Story*, *The Southern Review*, and *The Threepenny Review*. He currently teaches fiction writing and directs the Creative Writing Program at Trinity University in San Antonio, Texas.

Raphael Rae is a poet, essayist, painter, body horror enthusiast, and crazy transsexual. Their writing appears or is forthcoming in *Delicate Friend*, *Entropy*, *Passages North*, and elsewhere. Originally from Philadelphia, they now reside in Brooklyn.

Hannah Sward's work has been widely published in literary journals in the US, Canada, and the UK. She has been a regular contributor at *Erotic Review* since 2015 and was Editor and Columnist at *Third Street Villager Los Angeles* and contributing writer at *The Fix* and *YourTango*. Hannah is on the board of Right To Write Press, a nonprofit that supports emerging writers who are incarcerated. She is the author of *Strip: A Memoir* (September 2022, Tortoise Books) which has received rave reviews from authors such as Melissa Broder, Caroline Leavittt, and Noble Prize winner, J.M. Coetzee.

Jodie Noel Vinson (Susan Atefat Prize for Creative Nonfiction) holds an MFA in creative nonfiction from Emerson College. Her essays have been published in *Harvard Review*, *The New York Times*, *Ploughshares*, *Literary Hub*, *Creative Nonfiction*, *Agni*, *The Rumpus*, and *Electric Literature*, among other places. She lives in Providence, where she is writing a book about the creative expression of chronic illness.

John Sibley Williams is the author of nine poetry collections, including *Scale Model of a Country at Dawn* (Cider Press Review Poetry Award), *The Drowning House* (Elixir Press Poetry Award), *As One Fire Consumes Another* (Orison Poetry Prize), and *Skin Memory* (Backwaters Prize, University of Nebraska Press). His book *Sky Burial: New & Selected Poems* is forthcoming in translation from by the Portuguese press do lado esquerdo. A twenty-seven-time Pushcart nominee, John is the winner of numerous awards, including the Wabash Prize for Poetry, Philip Booth Award, Phyllis Smart-Young Prize, and Laux/Millar Prize. He serves as editor of *The Inflectionist Review* and founder of the Caesura Poetry Workshop series.

Jane Zwart teaches at Calvin University, where she also co-directs the Calvin Center for Faith & Writing. Her poems have appeared in *Poetry, The Southern Review, Threepenny Review, TriQuarterly*, and *Ploughshares,* as well as other journals and magazines. She also writes book reviews, most recently for *Plume* and *Tupelo Quarterly,* and she's published edited versions of onstage interviews with writers including Zadie Smith, Amit Majmudar, and Christian Wiman.

25TH ANNUAL ARTS & LETTERS PRIZES

2023 SUBMISSIONS OPEN:
FEBRUARY 1st — MARCH 31st

OUR READERS

POETRY

MER ALSOBROOKS ❖ DARIAN ARAIZA-SAMPLES
KIERAN BINNEY ❖ KELSIE DORAN ❖ AUDEN EAGERTON
SHERRI-ANNE FORDE ❖ AVERY JAMES ❖ NATALIE MAU

FICTION

COLIN BISHOFF ❖ TIMOTHY CONNORS ❖ RACHEL KERGER
ARON LIEBIG ❖ KELLY PIGGOT ❖ DENECHIA POWELL
COURTNEY SCHMIDT ❖ WILLIAM WARREN

CREATIVE NONFICTION

PAUL BRYANT ❖ MADELINE DAVIS ❖ MEGAN DUFFEY
JONNA SMITH ❖ SHANNON YARBROUGH